About the Author

Don Aslett, America's foremost authority on 'clean', has been advising Americans since 1981 how to kick kitchen grease out forever, whittle the wax buildup off floors and furniture, and sweeten the stalest atmosphere. For 33 years he and the professional cleaning company he founded, Varsity Contractors, have cleaned in every situation and setting imaginable, commercial and domestic—bachelor pads and eight-child homes; boats, planes, and buses; hotels, schools, offices, and factories; log cabins and million-dollar mansions; they've even cleaned up after fires, floods and tornadoes.

He's shared the how-tos of it all with the world in nine books. His first best-seller, *Is There Life After Housework?*, a primer of professional cleaning methods for the homemaker, has sold over half a million copies and been translated into five languages.

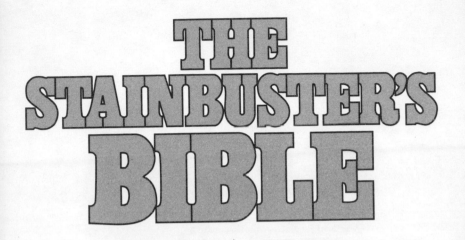

DON ASLETT

EBURY PRESS
LONDON

Published in Great Britain by Ebury Press
an imprint of the Random Century Group Ltd
Random Century House, 20 Vauxhall Bridge Road, London SW1V 2SA

First impression 1991

First published in the USA by New American Library

British Library Cataloguing in Publication Data
Aslett, Don *1935* –
  Stainbuster's bible.
  1. Fabrics. Stains. Removal
  I. Title
  648.1

  ISBN 0–85223–996–3

Edited by Elizabeth Martyn
Designed by Gwyn Lewis
Illustrations by Craig LaGory

Typeset in Plantin by Textype Typesetters, Cambridge
Printed and bound in Great Britain

Contents

Note to Readers

If I've learned anything in more than thirty years of professional cleaning, it's that even using the best available methods and materials, in the most ordinary cleaning situations, the result can sometimes boomerang. So don't expect perfection, in this volume or anywhere else.

If you bought a book on sex, cooking, or raising children, and it promised that after you'd read and applied it you'd never have a bad night or a sunken cake, or that your children would do as they were told for the rest of their lives—you wouldn't believe it. There are too many things information alone can't predict or control. I've tried a never-fail barbecued peach crumble recipe seven times now, for example, and each time that crumby, charcoaly mass has come out worse than the time before. My wife and I had eight teenagers at home all at once not so long ago, and need I tell you that neither the best book nor a master's in child management could guarantee results.

So it is with spot and stain removal. I've known stains come out in seconds, when under different conditions I couldn't get the very same stain off with sandpaper!

In these pages I've provided the best of my own third-of-a-century of stain and spot removal experience, and that of a wide variety of other stain veterans, but I still can't promise every carpet, sofa or T-shirt will come up completely clean, every time. I can only guarantee that the odds for successful removal and of avoiding harm to the garment or surface will swing in your favour. It's as if you called the doctor and said, 'I don't feel well, Doctor, what should I do?' 'What's wrong?' 'Well, I think it's my elbow again.' What the doctor tells you to do depends a lot on **your** judgement and assessment of what's wrong. Likewise, spots and stains are hard to diagnose via the printed page. I've tried to give you enough information to make the chances of recovery pretty promising. But just like the doctors, I do have to disclaim. I won't get the glory for your stainbusting triumphs, and, unfortunately, I can't take responsibility for your failures, either.

Good Spotting,

Don Aslett

Introduction

There's a Stain Out There with Your Name on It!

'Help! My husband sweats heavily and the armpits of his leather coat are incredibly stained. How do I get it out?'

I've done several thousand radio and television interviews on cleaning, and no matter what I'm supposed to be discussing—floors, walls, bathroom cleaning, or clutter—I inevitably get questions like that. I can attempt to switch the conservation back to beating rugs, but once the stain bug is out, all the calls—at least ten in a row—are on spills, spots, stains, and the odours they create. I finally realised why—stains and spots are the casualty ward of cleaning. All other cleaning can wait if it has to. General cleaning can be pretty low key, but not stains and spots. They always happen at the wrong time and in the wrong place, and we can't say I'll call back later. If they stay, they set and ruin things, and we get tired of converting £20 shirts to workshirts.

We can fake, gloss, and smooth our way over most unpleasant events—but not a stain. It talks to us: 'Well, clumsy, how are you going to tackle this?'

Here's some help!

In a lifetime we can expect to deal with an average of 50,000 spots, stains and spills.

The Queen can just move to a new castle if she spills custard on the carpet. If Madonna had a stained blouse, a million teenagers would try to copy it! And Rupert Murdoch can simply buy a new building with a dry cleaners on the ground floor.

Unfortunately, most of us can't pull off those tricks. We're stuck with the stains. All of which will come at the worst possible time, and end up in the worst possible place. We all know how many seemingly innocent stainmakers are out there, just itching for a chance to jump on us. Just as we know the bread always falls butter side down, we know how it is with stains.

* They happen as soon as something comes back from the cleaners, not before it goes in.
* We get them on the way to work, never on the way home.
* A stain will never hit a sleeve, if a crotch or a bosom is available.
* It's always in the middle, never on the edge.
* The red candles never drip until they're on Aunt Emily's lace tablecloth.
* The baby won't feel like puking until we get dressed up.
* Bloody beef or overripe melon will be served on a one-ply paper plate.
* The microwave meal that explodes on opening will be the one with indelible sauce.
* Nobody ever slops red wine on to a burgundy rug.
* Cars miss mud puddles until we walk past.
* Nosebleeds know when you're wearing Dry Clean Only.
* We won't brush up against the door latch unless we're wearing a white linen skirt.
* Cooking grease always finds the part of our anatomy the apron doesn't cover.
* Mayonnaise only squirts out of a sandwich when it really matters.
* The boss will bring up your future with the company over the sweet-and-sour spare ribs.
* The pizza topping won't land on the photocopy.
* The spot will be in the part that you iron last.

And on top of all that, we don't get the old, easy stains of our forefathers, we get space-age spots! We've developed more spot and stain sources since 1935 than they had in all 13,975 years previous (even counting chariot axle grease).

Not too long ago, mud, grass, grease and cocoa were about it. Today, we come up against thousands of chemicals, hundreds of drinks, inks, paints, sprays, foods, condiments, coatings, lubricants, and cosmetics. Spots and stains are as inevitable as flu and VAT—and no one is exempted. They hit the rich as well as the poor, and observe true equality of sexes as they follow us faithfully from the cradle to the nursing home. If we don't cause it, someone else will spill it on us or our property. No life is secure enough, no possession so well hidden it can escape the long arms of stains. We have cells and corpuscles to help get germs and viruses out of our life, but there's nothing that wades in when the splat of

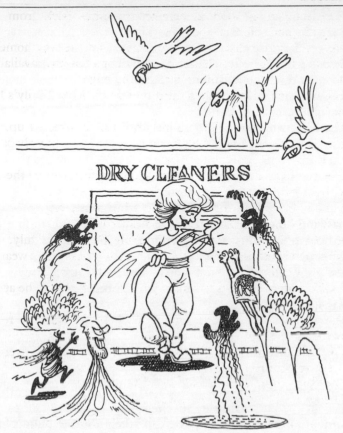

cheesecake lands in our lap. When it comes to spots and stains, we're on our own as soon as they land on us!

The Stainbuster's Bible to the Rescue! Dropping your coffee cup is a lot like falling off a bike—it's the landing that hurts, not the fall. Quick, expert first aid is the answer to both. In the case of stains, if you know what to use and how to use it you can minimise, if not eliminate, the damage. With the information in this little volume, anyone can become an expert at removing common, everyday stains. Just knowing what to do and doing it in time makes most spots easy to manage.

And once you've learned how to get them out:

★ You won't have to wait for a week to wear it or get it back from the cleaners.

11

★ You can cope when disaster strikes the only white shirt you packed for a business trip, or your party dress when you haven't even reached the party.

★ There's a much better chance of actually getting a stain out if you can do it yourself there and then. Time sets most stains, and some spots, if you can't get to the dry cleaner fast enough to avoid permanent damage.

★ Even if a stain needs a pro, you'll know what to do to keep it from getting worse while help is on the way.

★ You'll save money by not rushing everything down to the dry cleaners. They deserve your business, but for all your spots? Impossible! Not to mention all the money that won't be lost on ruined garments, finishes, and furnishings.

★ Knowing how to handle stains at home or away can do a lot for human relations, too. (Including all those stains made by guests or visiting children.)

★ You'll save time, mental anguish, and embarrassment.

★ There's a lot of pride and satisfaction in being able to do your own stainbusting, too!

So you can grin and wear it, or grin and remove it. You really can. Does it take a lot of knowledge and specialised chemicals to do this?

No, the instructions for removing each kind of stain are easy to follow and don't call for any special experience. The spotting equipment is all available at chemists, hardware shops or department stores. In these pages I'll teach you the secrets and techniques of the experts, the people who are up against serious stains every day—dry cleaners, professional launderers, carpet-cleaning technicians, chemists, manufacturers, and mothers. I'll even tell you when to give up and call in the cavalry, or toss it into the dressing-up box! But with a little care and practice, anyone can learn to take care of most spots and spills. Before you know it, you'll find yourself skilfully removing stains that once made you fear and tremble. And you'll be amazed how many blotches are childsplay to remove!

Are You Stain-Prone?

(Check your stain quotient—do you have spotability?)

A five-minute test to determine how many stains you invite daily. Tick any of the following that you do.

- ☐ Own skirts/dresses/dressing gowns that reach the ground
- ☐ Own anything white, yellow, or pale orange
- ☐ Have floors of unfinished wood, or unsealed concrete
- ☐ Don't use, or believe in, Scotchgard
- ☐ Have any unmended leaks
- ☐ Leave half-full cups or tins around
- ☐ Feed pets in unauthorised places (at least sometimes)

- ☐ Think aprons are sissy
- ☐ Put half-eaten chocolate bars on the dashboard or seat of the car
- ☐ Choose raspberry or cherry every time
- ☐ Kneel on the freshly cut lawn
- ☐ Try to carry bulging shopping bags one-handed
- ☐ Leave anything open on the stairs
- ☐ Believe there's anywhere you can put the nail polish bottle down that's 'spill proof'
- ☐ Lose the lid of anything
- ☐ Move a ladder with something on it
- ☐ Chew gum
- ☐ Smoke (you're guilty of at least thirty stains already)
- ☐ Lose pen caps the first day you use them
- ☐ (For men only) Overshoot the bowl
- ☐ 'Forget' to put down old newspapers before you clean the oven
- ☐ Like extra-long trousers or cuffs
- ☐ Have soup-dip length hair, beard, or moustache
- ☐ Decide to pick something up later
- ☐ Wear white or suede shoes
- ☐ Can't be bothered to change into 'painting clothes'
- ☐ Eat in traffic
- ☐ Eat while reading or working with papers
- ☐ Eat in the living-room
- ☐ Eat over carpet, anywhere
- ☐ Eat while half-asleep
- ☐ Eat on the sly, or pick at leftovers
- ☐ Eat in bed or while lying down
- ☐ Eat from a tray on your lap
- ☐ Buffet-style eating
- ☐ Eat in cars, boats, or anything in motion
- ☐ Eat without a napkin, or with too small a napkin
- ☐ Eat without leaning forward
- ☐ Don't bother to wipe your fingers after eating finger foods
- ☐ Gobble up any greasy snack food

Give yourself one point per tick, and add up your score.
1–10 = We should all lead such a spotless life.
11–20 = I'm glad to see you only spend about half your time removing spots.
21–30 = Hope your dog is called Spot!
31–40 = You'll be reincarnated as a leopard.

How to Use This Book

There are other books on stains, but this one's different. Yes, the step-by-step procedures you need to remove life's most annoying stains are in here (in Part III, 'How to Go About It'). And I've introduced you to all the stainbusting techniques you need to act effectively when a stain happens. There are lists and descriptions of the tools and chemicals you need to be a real stain pro, and a professional rating of home remedies for stains that often just make things worse. But a lot of these pages are devoted to helping you avoid all this work completely!

Part I, for example, takes a hard look at stains and how they happen. It explains the simple rules for keeping ordinary spills from developing into problem stains. It gives you a guided tour of the whole landscape of stains, and tells you how to make expert use of an ordinary old washing machine to dispose of three-quarters of them. It lets you know when the wisest move is to take it to the pros—or chuck it in the bin. It tells you how to protect your clothing and other possessions from stain damage, and even how to *prevent* the most common and dangerous stains.

Part II is a directory of the different kinds of surfaces where stains occur, and how to handle each one. Because the stain is only half the story. The other, equally important half, is what's it **on**? There's a world of difference in handling a tomato sauce stain if it's on a white cotton blouse, a nylon carpet, or a quarry-tiled floor. Before you start to remove a stain, don't just look up the procedure for that specific stain in 'How to Go About It'. Look up the particular surface it's on, too, in Part II. This will tell you what to do and what not to do to that specific material, to avoid damage and disappointment. This section also gives you insight into the relative stain-resistance of different fabrics, furnishings and building materials, to help you choose the ones that will keep you out of trouble.

I put Part III, 'How to Go About It,' at the end of the book, to help persuade you to read the other parts first. I know how you would-be stainbusters think! You buy the book as a hedge against the day you drop the borscht on the dining-room rug. But you don't read it, because who can tell what the big spill will be—it might be chocolate ice cream or claret. No sense in boning up on borscht now, you may never get a chance to apply all the hard-earned knowledge. So you put the book on the shelf, and

15

when the crisis occurs, you grab it and turn to "B" for borscht. Right? Wrong! If you read at least Part I now, you may avoid catastrophe altogether, or at least make it less of a mess when it does happen. Equip yourself with all the important background information **now**—not when you're up to your ankles in beetroot soup. I can just see you sitting there asking yourself: 'I wonder what "tamp" means, and what do "feathers" have to do with all this?' So do yourself a favour. Read at least Part I, and maybe even Part II, and start assembling the tools and chemicals you'll need to be prepared. I don't expect you to sit down and read through all the 'How to Go About It's' for everything from Acid to Wood Stain, but I hope you really will read the rest. Then, when the big spill happens, you'll be ready for it.

Speaking of Part III, I've tried to simplify it so that it isn't full of repetitive instructions. There are only so many ways to remove a stain, and a lot of different stains are handled the same way. So I've bunched the ones that are treated alike together. Lipstick and shoe polish are both removed the same way, for instance, so they both appear under one procedure. The easiest way to find the removal instructions for a particular stain is to look that stain up in the index. All the stains in the book are listed there and cross-referenced, to make them easy to find.

I've also geared the instructions in Part III toward the items we're most often trying to clean, and that generally turns out to be clothing. We spill a lot of stuff on carpets, too, for example, but we're not too keen on getting down on our hands and knees to clean them up. Unless a carpet spill is really noticeable, we often just walk on it for a while, until it blends in, and then try to hold out until the steam-cleaning man comes. But let us get a smudge or spot on our white linen jacket or Liberty print silk tie, and it's instant stain warfare—can't have something around that makes such an obvious statement about our character, can we? And that's why many of the stain removal instructions are slanted towards spots on garments. It's easy to adjust the procedures for use on other surfaces, though, with the information in Part II.

That takes care of my part, the rest is up to you. Happy stainbusting!

PART I

STAINBUSTER'S BASICS

1 Don't Do That!

The Mistakes That Turn Tiny Spots into Big Stains

You had a tiny leak in your tyre and you **ignored it**, so you had a blowout or a ruined tyre. You tried to mop the floor without sweeping it, and ended up with mud and stock-cube smears. You didn't **remove the worst of it first**. You put lawn-mower fuel in a water jug, only to grab it when you wanted a drink, or to put out a fire. It's the **wrong stuff**! And who could forget the doctor who didn't **pre-test** the patient, and amputated the wrong arm. Then there was that small, itchy spot you couldn't refrain from **rubbing** into a raging rash. What about the time you ended up with an aquarium full of boiled goldfish before you realised the **heating setting** was wrong?

Your own life experience has already exposed you to the six deadly sins that make a stain worse. Let's take a closer look at them so we can keep those spots small!

The Six Deadly Sins—Guaranteed to Turn a Simple Spot into a Sinister Stain

Ignoring it. Almost every stain is easier to remove when fresh. (The exceptions are things like mud, which is best left to dry, so that most of the mess can be dry-brushed away.) But for most stains, the quicker you get started on them, the better your chance of success. A cola spill on the carpet is no problem if you blot it up the minute it happens. If you let it go, the liquid soaks into the fibres and seeps down into the backing and underlay, and the sugars and caramel colouring set into a stain that won't be easy to remove, especially from the depths of the carpet. The same is true of pet stains. If treated immediately with the right product (see pp. 47 and 165), all traces can be eliminated, but an old, dried pet stain in carpet is all but impossible to remove.

Alcoholic drinks spilled on clothing can damage the fabric and be impossible to remove if left to dry (especially on wool)—which is why you should always sponge alcohol spills off with water immediately. Ditto for coffee, cologne, perfume, and milk. Most oils (salad oil, mayonnaise, margarine, motor oil) will oxidise and set within a matter of days if not removed. When Puss eats a dead mouse and brings it up on the tracksuit you left on the bathroom floor, the impulse is to bundle it up and bury it in the bottom of the dirty clothes basket. But you need to take a deep breath and rinse it out *now*—otherwise those strong stomach acids will bleach and permanently sully your sweats. **Quick action** is the single most important rule in spot removal—get 'em before they have a chance to become stains.

Not removing the worst of it first. Why launch into chemical warfare on any part of a stain or spill if you can just sweep, scrape, or vacuum it away? The easily removable part is usually the **bulk** of it. Whether it's liquid or solid, get up as much as you can before using any spotters, even water. Remember: spotters are solvents, made to **dissolve** the stain. If you have a blob of tar or grease on your coat, the last thing to do is apply solvent before removing as much of the tar or grease as you can. The dyes in a dab of tar, lipstick, or blusher can stain a huge area if you dilute with solvent and start spreading it around. So remove as much of the deposit as possible while it's dry and intact, then use water or solvent to remove what little remains. It's amazing how much you can get out just by gently working it and being patient, before ever adding liquid of any kind.

With liquid spills, too—why try to chemically counteract 8 oz of baby food when you could blot 7½ oz up first? Liquid spills should be blotted up, and solids can be gently scraped up with a blunt knife or spoon, or brushed off. Brittle residues can often be coaxed out by flexing the fabric—folding it over sharply in the area of the stain and rubbing it back and forth on itself. Fresh oily residues can be drawn out with an absorbent compound such as cat litter. Powders, such as photocopier toner, should be vacuumed. If you apply a liquid to unremoved powder, you're going to witness a spreading of your spot! It's like putting water on dirt— you end up with mud. But do take care not to smear any loose substances around or drive them into the fabric in your attempts to remove them.

Using the wrong stuff. I've done it dozens of times—got food, ink, or an airline terminal smudge on my suit or shirt when travelling, and as soon as I get to the hotel, rubbed a bar of soap on it and started scrubbing viciously. Then I give up, let it dry and take it home, and that stain is there for good!

It's critical to identify correctly what caused a stain and the material it's on before your start smothering it with chemicals. Ammonia can work wonders on blood and protein stains, but it can set coffee and make it permanent. Acetone will dissolve nail

polish out of many fabrics, but will melt a hole in your acetate slip. Chlorine bleach can be very helpful for man-made fibres, but will attack silk and wool. Alcohol will bleed dyes from some fabrics. Even water will set many oily stains, such as salad dressing and mustard. Take the time to be sure of what caused the stain—don't just jump to conclusions—whether you plan to work on it yourself, or take it to a pro. The care labels in clothes should tell you the type of fabric you're dealing with and how to handle it (see p. 94).

PRE-TEST

Forgetting to pre-test. With hundreds of different fibres and blends around today, it's sometimes hard to be sure what you're dealing with. So it's always a good idea to test (*that means practice, or experiment with!*) any spotting chemical in an inconspicuous area to make sure it won't damage the fabric or cause the colour to change. Even plain water will draw the dye out of some silks, and it's better to have something like that happen in the seam allowance or hem of a garment than smack in the middle of it. Test carpet on a remnant, or in a cupboard or other out-of-the-way place; test upholstered furniture on the back or underside.

Rubbing and scrubbing it. The first thing most of us want to do with a stain—it helps us feel as if we're doing something. But it's dangerous for two reasons: it spreads the stain, and it can damage the surface from which we're trying to remove the stain. We've all done it—started out with a pen mark or grease spot so tiny, we're almost tempted to leave it alone, no one will notice. But it's like a scab or a missing chip of paint, we just can't let it be. Now it's noticeable, we know it was a bad move, so more speed, solution, and pressure. Before you know it, we've rubbed the paint or finish off!

We should remove stains by gently drawing the staining agent out of the fabric, by blotting and flushing. If something more than that is needed, we use a gentle 'tamping' or special scraping technique (see Chapter 5). Vigorous rubbing or scrubbing usually just makes a stain bigger, more obvious and harder to remove. Scrubbing will often bruise the fabric or fibres, too, leaving a pilled or fuzzy spot where you worked on it—or, if the fabric is delicate, even a hole. These scrubbed spots will show and look bad, even if you get all the stain out, because the surface has been roughened and damaged. Avoid wringing stained fabrics too, because this can distort the fabric as well as drive the stain deeper into the fibres.

Applying heat. Many stains are 'set' by heat. An otherwise removable stain will become impossible to shift when washed in hot water, dried in the tumble dryer, or ironed. When you're working on a stain, use a cold or warm water wash, and check to make sure that the stain has come out before throwing the item into the dryer. And if you wash your white socks with a red sweatshirt and get a 'pink load,' don't dry it (see p. 33). Always inspect 'removed' stains carefully before ironing—the heat will often oxidise any remaining residue and turn it yellow.

Don't help innocent spots develop into permanent stains! Handling everyday spots and spills successfully doesn't take an expert, just somebody like you with a little common sense and a slower trigger finger.

Never

★ Ignore a stain or leave it until 'later'

★ Fail to take advantage of the fact that three-quarters or more of the stain or spot can probably be swept, scraped, or vacuumed away

★ Apply water or any chemical until you're sure you know what the stain is and what it's on

★ Forget to pre-test

★ Rub or scrub a stain

★ Apply heat of any kind to a stain that hasn't been removed 100 per cent

---

2 It Might Come Out in the Wash

Wash It Out—the Basic Stain Removal Strategy for Washables

If most of the clothes you wear are washable, the majority of your stain skirmishes will be won or lost in the utility room. Three out of four everyday stains can simply be washed out, if you just take a little extra time to identify and pre-treat spots before you toss everything in. For washables, this is the easiest way to deal with all but problem stains. For fabrics and colours that tolerate hot water and chlorine bleach, even a lot of the tough stains will come out in the washing machine, including alcoholic drinks, coffee, milk, ice cream, cosmetics, grass stains, chocolate, egg, fruit juice, and gravy.

Here's how to build effective stain removal into your laundry routine:

Stay aware of stains. And make sure anyone else whose clothes you wash makes you aware of them, so you can give them special attention. The heat of washing or drying will otherwise make many stains impossible to get out.

Don't wait until washday. Most spots become more stubborn with age, and some are hard to see after they dry, so the safest approach is to tend to spots and spills as soon as they happen. Wash the garment immediately if at all possible, because there's less chance of success with each passing day. It's worth a wash to save a £20 pair of trousers after a brush with barbecue sauce (and there's always *something* in the laundry basket that could safely be used to make up the load). That greasy red stain will only cost you a few minutes and about 30p to remove—what a bargain. If you can't wash straight away, sponge fresh stains with plain water. At the very least, stick a safety pin on the spot, so that you remember that the sweater you're washing on Saturday still has half of Thursday's milkshake spilled down the front.

★ When you come upon a stain, remember: **always get rid of the worst of it first!** Knock it off, scrape it off, or brush it off. Gobs of grease, lumps of manure, and crusts of mud don't disappear in the wash, they're dissolved and circulated—so the less there is on a garment, or on anything being cleaned, the better the end result.

Pre-treat! Most stains on washable items will benefit from pre-treatment (as described for each specific stain in Part III of this book—'How to Go About It'), followed by washing in warm water. You can pre-treat while you're sorting the loads, as you're going through pockets, etc. This will give the pre-treatment the few minutes it needs to sit before you load the machine (see p. 30 for more on pre-treatments).

Pre-soak problem items you come across, if indicated in the instructions for that stain.

Don't overload your machine. All the detergent and pre-treatment in the world can't get stains out (and clothes clean) if there isn't room for the agitator to do its job—flush water thoroughly through the fabric.

Don't use hot water unless the instructions for that stain specifically call for it (see opposite).

Use chlorine bleach if the fabric will tolerate it. It's much better at removing stains than the milder bleaches (but read the warnings on pp. 28/29 and 43/44 first).

Check to see if the stain is still there after laundering—then re-treat and wash again if necessary. Even if you think it's gone, air dry the item and have another look. Don't use any heat (such as tumble drying or ironing) until you're sure it's 100 per cent removed. Heat will set many stains and make them permanent.
★ If this doesn't get it, try the specialised spot removers and techniques in 'How to Go About It,' then wash again.

Detergent Strategy for Stainbusting

All washing powders do a superior job of removing everyday soil compared to the plain soap we used to use, but in taking out stains, you'll probably notice a difference if you use the most effective products available. Liquid detergents such as Ariel, Daz and Persil liquids are great for removing normal soil and especially good at keeping nylons white, but they don't remove make-up, ink, and oil stains as well as the powdered detergents, which are usually cheaper, too. Bold is an excellent oil stain remover, though it, too, doesn't whiten nylon as well. Enzyme (biological) detergents do a better job on protein stains such as grass, egg, blood, and gravy. For all-around soil removal, effectiveness on stains, and reasonable price, it's still hard to beat good old Daz or Surf.

Washing detergent contains surfactants and emulsifiers to lift off and wash away greasy soils, so pre-treating with detergent (mixed into a paste with water, if it's the powdered type) or even laundering alone will remove some of the easier grease stains.

Water Temperature Wisdom

Without a doubt, detergents and bleaches work better in hot water than they do in cold. But when stain removing, it's generally better to wash everything in warm water. This gives the best possible cleaning action while avoiding heat-setting the stains. Only greasy stains are washed in hot, and only certain stains, such as blood and egg, are washed in cold. (See individual instructions for each stain in 'How to Go About It.') A cold-water wash will also minimise shrinking if you're working with washable woollens, and avoid dye loss in very bright or dark colours.

For most efficient stain-removal and, for that matter any other washing, all rinses should be in cold water. It saves energy and reduces wrinkling, too.

To Bleach or Not to Bleach

Bleach is one of the big guns of stain removal—but treat it with respect. There are two types commonly used for home laundry: liquid chlorine (household) bleach, such as Parazone, Domestos, Vortex or 'own brand' chlorine bleaches, and oxygen bleach, such as Eco or Ark products, Asda non-chlorine products, or use hydrogen peroxide. Chlorine is unquestionably the better stain remover, but it's a powerful bleach that has to be used carefully to avoid fabric or colour damage. Oxygen bleach is much milder and can be used safely on all washable fabrics, but it requires hot water to be of much use—it's only marginally effective in warm water, and almost useless in cold. Chlorine bleach does a good job in warm water and fairly well in cold.

Repeated use of chlorine bleach in too strong a concentration on cotton and other natural fibres can weaken the fabric. Wool and silk are destroyed by chlorine bleaches. Before you know it, you'll be finding holes and faded colours in cotton and cotton-blend fabrics. But occasional use of chlorine bleach can work wonders in removing stubborn stains. If it isn't used too often and if it's diluted properly, it shouldn't harm bleach-safe fabrics.

Chlorine bleach is generally safe for white or colourfast fabrics except wool, silk, mohair and certain flame-retardant finishes—check the label.

Quick Henry, the Bleach!

Bleach isn't an only child, there's a whole family of bleaches. Here are the ones I recommend for stain removal, listed in order from strongest to weakest.

Chlorine bleach (sodium hypochlorite). Generally a liquid, such as Domestos or Parazone. A good stain remover, but this is powerful stuff that has to be used with great care because it can damage skin and household surfaces (see pp. 28/29).

Colour remover. Designed to remove fabric dyes before re-dyeing, it can be a big help in getting rid of unwanted colours and dye stains, especially, eg Dygone Run Away. But it must be stored and handled cautiously (see p. 46).

Hydrogen peroxide. Can serve as a mild bleach that's safe for almost any fabric. Available from chemists.

Oxygen or 'all-fabric' bleach (sodium perborate). Available in some powder formulations (see opposite), this is a much milder bleach than chlorine and it needs hot water (which we don't often use in stain removal) to do its best work. It won't get as many of the spots out, but it's safer to use and safer for fabrics and surfaces. And it can be used to make a paste for spot bleaching.

Lemon juice and vinegar. Are mild acids that have a gentle, safe bleaching action, as freckle-fighting redheads always knew.

Ammonia. Also has a mild bleaching action, useful on acid-sensitive fabrics such as cotton and linen.

 This symbol indicates that household (chlorine) bleach could be used. Care must be taken to follow the bleach manufacturer's instructions.

 When this symbol appears on a label, household bleach must not be used.

If in doubt, test first by mixing one tablespoon of chlorine bleach in one-quarter cup water. Put a drop of this solution on hidden part of the item, leave it for a minute, and blot it out. If there's no colour change, it's safe to bleach.

Always dilute liquid bleach according to directions, and be sure to measure accurately. Never put undiluted bleach directly on to anything. Be sure to mix it in with the water before you add your laundry. Chlorine bleach is very corrosive to metals and reacts strongly with acids and some alkalis to form poisonous chlorine gas, so always be careful how and where you use it. For stain removal on fabrics not safe for chlorine bleach, and for everyday laundry, use one of the safer oxygen (all-fabric) bleaches.

A Word About Fabric Conditioner Spots

Fabric conditioners coat the fibres of fabric with a lubricating film that helps them drape better, wrinkle less, feel softer, and attract less lint (by reducing static cling). This is all fine and desirable, but be sure to follow the drying temperature directions, especially for synthetics. The chemical in conditioning sheets used in tumble dryers can leave oily spots on man-made fibres at high heat settings. The liquid fabric conditioners you add to the rinse water can also leave spots if they're poured directly on to clothes. To remove these spots, sponge with water, rub in detergent, and wash again.

The Fine Points of Pre-treating

Pre-treatments such as Frend, Shout, Vanish, Biotex and Fairy, are the modern launderer's best friend. They can be found as trigger and aerosol sprays and laundry 'bars.' Pre-treatments contain soil dissolvers that penetrate stubborn stains and suspend them in the water so they can be flushed away.

The big drawback of spray-on pre-treatments is: we want to treat a stain when it's fresh, but we don't want to stop and wash the item there and then. So we end up throwing it in the laundry basket untreated and wait until we do a wash to pre-treat. Some stains will set and become much harder to remove during that time.

The laundry bars may be a little less powerful than the sprays, but they do have certain advantages. You can treat a stain immediately, then wait up to a week to wash. Some people keep a laundry bar by the laundry basket and routinely dab any stains as they throw the dirty clothes in (what a great trick to teach your children). The bar pre-treatment won't dry out before your week is up, and the soil will still be softened, suspended, and ready to wash out when you get round to doing the washing.

Different pre-treatments have different formulas, and vary in how well they work on specific stains. Most of them will improve everyday grass, blood, food, and beverage stains, and oily stains like dressings and gravy. Some will take out one type of stain much better than another.

Laundry pre-treatments shouldn't be used for spot removal on carpet, upholstery, dry-cleanable garments, or anything else that can't be laundered.

No matter what type of pre-treatment you use: treat the whole spot, not just the middle or most of it. It wouldn't hurt to overlap a little on to the unspotted fabric beyond, especially for thick or aged spots. Work it in a little after you put it on; and bear in mind that some stains may need a second treatment and a second wash.

Stain Zones

These are the parts of clothing especially prone to stains, that need to be scanned every time we do a wash.

Ring around the... Collars, cuffs (and hatbands, too) get hair and skin oil and, in the case of shirt cuffs, a lot of up-against-whatever-we're-working-on staining. Check collars for shaving-cut blood specks, too.

The turn-ups or hems of light-coloured trousers, especially, are often smeared with mud, road tar, or shoe polish.

The fronts or 'bib' sections of **shirts and tops** are the scene of most food and drink fumbles. Search for overlooked spills and unnoticed stains. Clear soft-drink and fruit-juice dribbles are hard to see, for example. If not completely removed before ironing or tumble drying, the sugar in stains like these can be heat-set and become permanent.

Underarms and other sweat-soak spots.

Elbows get a lot of lean-on and -into stains.

Knees (ground-in soil and grass stains).

Seat. As a professional cleaner of perching places I advise you to look closely at chairs and bus seats before you lower yourself into them. You'll be amazed what an assortment of gooey spots and

---

A Dozen Good Ways to Create Stains in Laundry

★ Failing to sort dirty washing into whites, dark colours, noncolourfast stuff, etc. Mother didn't make those piles for the fun of it.

★ Tossing the wrong thing in to 'make up a load' (you can never let your guard down on sorting).

★ Doing any laundry two hours before the trip, or in a great hurry.

★ Letting wet—or half-dry—clothes rest on top of each other for hours.

★ Doing the wash while the plumbing's being mended.

★ Using fabric conditioner sheets in too hot a dryer.

★ Leaving washing where the cat or dog can snuggle down in it.

★ Ignoring the fact that the washing machine or dryer has a rusty drum.

★ Using mildewed or dirty clothespegs.

★ Leaving the washing on the line for so long, the birds bomb it.

★ Locating the clothesline under a mulberry tree.

sticky stains can be transferred from seats to our skirts and trousers. If in doubt as to origin, treat these as 'mystery' stains (see pp. 156/157).

Other residents of the laundry basket worth casting a sharp eye over for stains: tablecloths, napkins, sheets, pillowcases, mattress pads, underwear, and socks that have been worn without shoes!

Dye Transfer in Laundry

Some dyes and fabrics get married and live happily ever after, but not a few of these unions end in divorce—or at least separation. When the dye bleeds out of a fabric in the wash, it's called 'fugitive

33

dye,' and this is one fugitive that almost always gets caught, usually by your treasured white linen blouse or one-of-a-kind T-shirt. Of all the dyes, red is the least colourfast, with blue and purple next in line (in case you need a good excuse to wear green or brown). But any dark or bright colour can bleed, and some fabrics tend to lose dye and pick up fugitive dye worse than others. Madras is notorious for dye bleeding, as are many silks and acetates, and nylon seems to have a knack for attracting whatever vagrant dye might be floating around.

Don't trust luck, intuition, or even labels when it comes to the question of how colourfast an item will be. The safest bet is to wash any new, coloured garment by itself until you get to know it. Never trust red garments in with other clothes—especially whites—even if they've been washed before. If you do get a 'pink load' (or light blue, or lavender), don't dry it. Keep it wet. Rewash in warm water with chlorine bleach for white or colourfast fabrics, products containing non-chlorine bleach, or hydrogen peroxide, for the rest. It may take several washings to completely remove the fugitive dye. If the colour doesn't come out, you may have to use a colour remover. Don't dry the load until the unwanted colour is gone.

Yellowing

Yellowing can be caused by many things: white cotton and linen tend to yellow if stored in the dark for long periods. This kind of yellowing will often come out with a hot-water wash in chlorine bleach. If you don't use enough detergent when you wash, or use too low a wash temperature, a gradual build-up of body oils will also yellow garments. A short or gentle wash cycle may also not be enough to remove all the dirt from heavily soiled laundry. This condition can usually be reversed by pre-soaking in an enzyme detergent and washing in a hot detergent solution or cooker enzyme preparation. Colour remover such as Dygone Run Away can be used on white fabrics that can't take bleach.

Another cause of yellowing is chlorine retention in bleach-sensitive fibres such as drip-dry and crease-resistant fabrics. Try a colour remover, but this condition often can't be reversed. Another irreversible type of yellowing is the kind caused by hanging whites with light-sensitive brighteners out in the sun to dry. If the care label says 'dry out of direct light' it means what it says. A garment with yellowed fabric brightener is never going to be sparkling white again.

Iron or manganese in the water supply can also cause yellow or brown stains on white fabrics. See p. 166 (Rust) for how to remove these.

Stain Removal Strategy When Laundering

★ Stay alert for stains—before you wash, dry or iron.

★ Wash it **now**—the sooner you get to it, the better your chances of washing it away.

★ Don't pop it in the machine until you've brushed or lightly scraped away as much of the stain as you can.

★ Pre-treat! (And wash the object shortly afterwards if using a spray pre-treatment.)

★ Pre-soak if Part III of the book tells you to.

★ Use **warm** water unless Part III tells you otherwise.

★ Use chlorine bleach if safe for the colour fabric.

★ Don't overload the machine!

---

3 The Old Standbys

From Soda Water to Hair Spray

If you've ever tried to cut something with a blunt knife, I'm sure you ended up with some ragged edges. But you may have managed to get the job done—it was better than nothing. That's how I classify many of the hints and tips in newspapers, books, and magazines—the home remedies for stain removal. These old wives' and old husbands' tales have been around a long time—and some for good reason. A few of them work pretty well. Vinegar and alcohol, for example, are staples even in the pro spotter's kit. Others work, but not as reliably or as well as widely available and inexpensive professional stain removal products. Not a few of the home brews, though they do remove stains, have side effects that only cause new problems. There are better, safer alternatives. At a pinch, a home remedy might be worth using if nothing else is at hand, but only if you pay strict attention to certain precautions. All the rest, sad to say, are a waste of time and energy. Let's take a look to see which are worthwhile and which to steer clear of, before getting into the serious business of stain removing.

What it is and what's in it	*What it does*	*Comments*
Soda water Carbonated water, citric acid	Acts as a very mild acid cleaner—slightly more effective than plain water for water-soluble stains	Save your money—vinegar and water is cheaper
Denture cleaning tablets Oxygen bleach (perborate)	Will remove coffee, tea, and juice stains from teacups	So will vinegar and most other bleaches
Hair spray Alcohol and other volatile solvents and resins	Dissolves ink (the cheaper brands of hair spray are better for this purpose)	Must be removed (laundered) afterwards or will stiffen fabric—okay to use as a wash pre-treatment for ink stains
Nail polish remover Amyl acetate, possibly acetone and oils	Will dissolve nail polish, and possibly model glue	Oily types will leave a stain. Never use acetone on acetate fabrics
Cola Phosphoric acid, sugar, colouring, and carbonated water	Acts as a mild acid cleaner for things like toilet bowls and whitewall tyres	Not as effective as a ordinary phosphoric acid cleaner, and the sugar and caramel in cola create stain problems of their own
Ashes Cigarette or cigar ashes, sometimes mixed with fats or oils	Combined with fats, ashes form a mild soap, which is also mildly abrasive, used to rub water rings off furniture.	Ashes also contain carbon, which will cause its own stains. Better to use cream metal polish or another clean abrasive on porous surfaces.

What it is and what's in it	*What it does*	*Comments*
Toothpaste		
Mild soap, with flavouring and abrasives	Acts as mild abrasive cleaner	But it's messier to use than a lot of other abrasives. And like any abrasive it can leave surfaces dull and scratched. Use it sparingly and gently and make sure it's the plain white kind
Peanut butter		
Peanuts, vegetable oil	The oil in peanut butter softens and lubricates hardened stains, such as chewing gum. And because peanut butter is pasty it can be applied almost like a poultice.	Leaves an oil stain of its own which must be removed
Salt		
Sodium chloride	Helpful in absorbing potentially damaging stains such as red wine	Must be applied immediately, then brushed and rinsed away when dry
Alcohol		
A powerful solvent, useful in removing many types of dye stains	Can also make fabric dyes run—particularly in silk and acetate—test before using	For stain removal use methylated spirit (buy the colourless variety) or surgical spirit
Lemon juice		
Citric acid	A mild bleach, useful in removing wine, rust and other stains	Test first before using on silk, wool, cotton, linen, rayon, or acetate
Vinegar		
Acetic acid	Neutralises alkaline stains and spotter residues, also acts as a mild bleach. Useful in many stain removal operations	Use **white** vinegar only for stain removing, and dilute with two parts water for use on cotton or linen; pre-test for dye change before using on coloured fabrics

What it is and what's in it	*What it does*	*Comments*
Baking soda Sodium bicarbonate	Neutralises acid stains (such as bowl cleaner stains) and acid solutions, absorbs odours, acts as a mild bleach and, mixed with water into a paste, serves as a mild abrasive cleanser	Rinse away powder after using and bear in mind that vigorous scrubbing with baking soda may dull glossy surfaces
Soap Real soap, such as Lux, Woolite, and most bath soaps, as opposed to detergent	Helpful in removing many types of stains. Penetrates and lifts soil and lubricates the cleaning process	Don't use soap on fruit stains—it will set them. And avoid soap with strong colourings, scents, skin conditioners, deodorisers, or other ingredients not 100 per cent helpful to the stain-removal process
Shaving cream Mild soap, glycerine, skin conditioners	About as effective as real soap, but messier	Forget it, unless squirting it out of the can gives you a thrill

4 Your Stainbusting Kit

The Tools of the Trade

Don't let this list of spotting tools and chemicals scare you off—
you can jump in wherever you like. There may be a couple of
dozen things here, but only a few of them are new to you, and
I bet you've got ten of them on the premises already! (It's enough
to make a stain shrink in horror.) Here's the key:

★★★**Must-haves.** You need these for even a bare-bones spotting
kit. Assemble what you already have, go out and get the rest,
and you'll be all set to start stainbusting.

★★**Welcome additions.** These will round out your kit and give
you what you need to handle most common stains.

★**The ultimate.** With just four further items you'll be like a pro.
Even the tough and exotic stains are within your reach.

Don't be put off by the idea of going to the chemist specially
to buy some 'amyl acetate' or 'acetone,' either. We spend weeks,
if not months, of our life battling against the damage and
embarrassment of stains—a few minutes and a pound or two
getting the right stuff will go a long way towards changing that.
Think of the time and money we spend on removing complexion
blemishes—the blotches on our clothes, floors and furniture are
almost as noticeable.

Why can't I just use a miracle all-in-one spot remover? We see
ads all the time for miracle stain-removing sticks, liquids, sprays,
and powders. They promise to remove virtually any stain like
magic, or your money back. Most of them are fine on a certain
range of stains, but none of them is good at everything. Different
types of stains call for different cleaning chemistry, and no one
product can do it all. If you find one that works unusually well
on a particular type of stain, add it to your spotting kit. Keep
the packaging and directions with the product so you have all the
info when you need it. But don't expect one chemical to handle
every stain.

Tools

★★★**Scraper.** Many spot-getting procedures in this book call for scraping. Professional spotters use a 'bone scraper' or spatula, which is made of bone, plastic, or metal. You might be able to get one at a hardware shop or janitorial supplier, which can be found in the Yellow Pages under that very heading. But for home use, a butter knife works perfectly—use the blade for scraping, and the handle for gentle agitation (see p. 55). Keep one in your spotting kit with a simple, straight handle and a smooth, blunt blade (no nicks or serrations). For fabrics you wouldn't want to scrape with even a blunt blade, you can use the bowl of a soup spoon. (For scraping technique, see p. 51.)

★★★**Clean white cloths.** You need **white** cloths for stain removal. Spotting chemicals can cause dyed fabrics to bleed or transfer colour, and white cloths allow you to keep an eye open for this. They also enable you to keep track of how much stain is coming out and when it stops coming out.

Your stain kit cloths must be not only white, but **absorbent**—and you'd be amazed how many inhabitants of the rag bag aren't.

For absorbency use cotton, which means cotton towelling, cotton T-shirts or cotton nappies. Old white linen napkins are good and absorbent, too. For many of the stain-removal procedures in this book, fold your cloth into a pad about the size of your hand and about a quarter-to half-an-inch thick. A hand towel folded to facecloth size fits this description nicely.

★★★**Spray bottle.** A plastic bottle with a 'trigger sprayer' like the type used for misting houseplants or spray cleaning. In stain removal, use this mainly for flushing, and if you like you can use a plastic squeeze bottle instead.

★★★**Spotting brush.** A professional spotting brush has short, closely set bristles for 'tamping' stains (see p. 55 for an explanation of this), and a scraper on the end of the handle. You can use any small brush that has not-too-long bristles all the same length—odd bristles poking out anywhere are likely to damage the fabric. The brush you use on lightweight fabrics shouldn't be as stiff as a spotting brush for carpet or upholstery. A soft or medium toothbrush works well for small stains on garments, but you'll need a larger brush for carpet stains and heavier use. If you want a genuine spotting brush, most janitorial suppliers have them.

Am Ex etc—don't leave home without it

You're out somewhere and 'splat'—a forkful of gooey, gravy-soaked mashed potato falls on your lap. Your first reaction is a glance to see if your balancing act was noticed. Then you want to act quickly, because if left, the mess will set, and if you try rubbing it away it will only penetrate deeper and spread farther. To remove it, use the tinest and finest scraper and dustpan around—a firm, water-proof, germproof credit card. With it, you can scoop up goop, stain, and even broken glass. I've fielded spilled trays in a second while an alarmed waiter searched for a broom. Credit cards are a cinch to clean off afterwards, too!

★★★**Nylon scrubbing pad.** Does a better and safer job than a brush when a scrubbing action is really needed, such as on hard surfaces. Available from hardware shops and supermarkets as plain nylon pads (such as Scotchbrite) or nylon-faced sponges. In either form, choose the safe-for-all-surfaces white nylon type, not a green or brown one.

A stainbuster knows that tools and working areas need to be clean, too. It's not going to help a bit to have the remains of last month's *coq au vin* catastrophe still stuck to the roots of our spotting brush when we go to tidy up the corner behind the chair where Mitzie had her six pups. Rinse brushes vigorously after use and hang to dry. When you use your tools on sticky stuff like nail polish or glue, wipe it off before it cements itself.

Keep your absorbing cloths nice and clean (they don't have to be snowy white, but **clean**). Drying them in a tumble dryer will help keep them soft and thirsty. And retire them when they get rank and stiff with stain.

Chemicals

★★★Ammonia. Some stains require a slightly alkaline spotting agent. Ammonia can also serve as a mild bleach. Buy plain household ammonia, available at chemists. Always pre-test before using ammonia, as it affects some dyes. If you note a colour change when using it, rinse with water, apply a few drops of white vinegar to neutralise the ammonia, then rinse again. Don't use ammonia on silk or wool unless absolutely necessary, and then only diluted with an equal amount of water. Where directions call for a mild solution, use 1 tablespoon of ammonia in half a cup of water. Don't inhale the fumes—we've all had at least one experience of taking a big deep sniff of ammonia—your nostrils don't need to go through it again. And don't get ammonia on your skin or in your eyes!

★★★Chlorine bleach. Liquid bleach, such as Domestos or Parazone. This is sodium hypochlorite, a potent bleach not recommended for everyday laundry because it tends to weaken natural fabrics such as cotton, but it can be a big help in stain removal. Don't ever use it on silk, wool or permanent press or flame-retardant fabrics. Always pre-test chlorine bleach before using, and be careful not to breathe the fumes or get it in your eyes or on your skin. Don't use metal spoons or containers for liquid chlorine bleach, and **never** mix it with any other cleaning chemical. Don't use it straight—dilute it as recommended on the bottle. Always rinse it out of the fabric immediately. Watch closely for colour change and rinse at once if you see any sign of a dye change. If possible, bleach the entire garment, not just the spot, to avoid uneven colour change.

★★★**Hydrogen peroxide.** A mild bleach, safe for all fabrics. Effective on a surprising number of stains, especially blood and scorch. Pre-test before using on coloured fabrics. Buy the 20 vol strength available from chemists, and use it diluted in six parts of water. Don't buy too much, as it loses strength when stored for long periods. Adding a few drops of ammonia accelerates the bleaching action of peroxide.

★★★**Synthetic bleaches.** All-fabric oxygen bleaches, such as contained in Ark or Eco products, are safe for all colourfast fabrics, and can be used in the wash or mixed with water to form a paste for spot bleaching. Not nearly as effective as chlorine bleach at removing stains.

★★★**Enzyme detergents.** Biological washing powders such as Ariel, Bold and own-brands can be used as laundry pre-soaks or made into pastes with water for spotting dry cleanables. Warm water makes them work better. For soaking almost anything except bloodstains, mix the detergent in warm water and soak for 30 minutes to an hour. To make a paste, mix equal parts powder and water and pre-test for colourfastness before using. Leave the paste on the spot for 15 to 30 minutes, but don't let it dry out. Rinse thoroughly. Don't use on wool or silk.

★★★**Laundry pre-treatments.** Can help to remove a great many spots, especially grease, in the course of ordinary washing. Pre-treatments are put on and allowed to soak a few minutes before washing. Examples are Shout, Frend, Vanish, Biotex, Fairy. Pre-treatments need to be rinsed or washed out, and shouldn't be allowed to dry on the fabric. Don't get them in your eyes, or on paint or plastic. (For more on pre-treatments see Chapter 2.)

★★★**Neutral detergent.** When a stain removal instruction calls for this, use a washing-up liquid which is not highly coloured, or a gentle liquid designed for washing clothes, like Stergene. Never use heavy-duty household cleaners, automatic dishwashing compounds, or laundry detergents—they're too alkaline and can set some stains.

★★★**Vinegar.** A mild (5 per cent) solution of acetic acid, vinegar is used on stains that call for an acid spotter. It's also used to neutralise some alkaline stains and spotting chemicals, and can even serve as a mild bleach. Vinegar is especially useful on silk and wool, which don't tolerate ammonia well. Avoid using it on cotton, linen or acetate. Use only **white** vinegar, not the coloured wine or cider types. When directions call for a mild solution, mix 1:4 with water. Vinegar may cause colour change in some dyes. If colour change occurs, rinse well with water, add a few drops of ammonia, then rinse again.

★★★**Water.** The great cleaning medium; most spotting procedures call for water at some point. Unless otherwise specified, this means water at room temperature. Water must be used sparingly on fabrics such as silk and rayon, which tend to water-spot, and on 100 per cent wool.

If you have hard water, you might want to use soft or distilled water for spotting, because the dissolved minerals in hard water not only interfere with the action of soaps and detergents, but leave whitish stains of their own.

Keeping the Scene of the Grime from becoming the Scene of the Crime

When mechanics work on our car, our biggest complaint is often not their work, or even their bill, but the grease, dirt, and damage on the car seat, floor, door handle, bonnet, steering wheel, and so on. All because they didn't protect it from their mending mess! How many times in your life (when trying to mend or clean something or remove a stain from it) have you inflicted more stain or damage on it than it had to begin with? Such as when you try to take the nail polish off the tabletop, and remove the varnish instead.

Removing stains involves chemicals and moisture, and in the process of drawing the stain out, we always push some of it through. And there's usually another stainable—carpet, flooring, wall, or underwear—waiting right behind or below to absorb the just-released problem. Such as when you use a solvent to remove a spot from your Levi's while your legs are still in them, and the solvent seeps through to your skin to give you an ugly rash.

You can't always slide a piece of glass or wood (the best things for the purpose) under an item when you're taking out a spot, but on almost anything, from a bedspread to a tablecloth, you can slip an absorbent towel or similar protector between your working area and the nearest surface.

★★Absorber. A granular or sawdust-like material used for blotting or soaking up fresh stains, especially grease and oil. Use cat litter for heavy stains like oil drips in the garage and on dark-coloured fabrics. Cornflour and talcum powder work too, but can be hard to remove from fabric. If left on long enough (several hours, to all day), an absorber can often remove an oil stain completely. Rub it in and let it sit for a while, then brush or vacuum off.

★★Alcohol. A powerful solvent that's especially useful for fabrics you can't use water on. For stain removal use colourless methylated spirit or surgical spirit. **CAUTION**: Alcohol can make dyes run, especially in silk and acetates, so always pre-test in an inconspicuous place. When using alcohol on acetates, always dilute it with two parts water. Alcohol is also **extremely flammable**, so don't use it around sparks or flame.

★★Colour remover. Designed to remove the **old** colour before re-dyeing fabrics, colour removers do indeed remove many dyes from white fabrics. Some desperate and courageous cleaners use colour removers successfully on colourfast dyed fabrics, too, but it's tricky. Colour remover can sometimes cause a radical colour change in coloured fabric (such as from green to orange!) If that happens, you may be able to return things to normal by rinsing immediately with water. Colours faded or bleached by colour remover, on the other hand, can't be restored. Dygone Run Away and Stain Devils Colour Run Remover are available at supermarkets. **Poisonous**: Always use according to directions.

Must-Haves for the Stainbuster's Kit

scraper
clean white cotton cloths
spray bottle or squeeze bottle
plain household ammonia
chlorine bleach
20 vol hydrogen peroxide
enzyme detergent
proprietary grease solvent
laundry pre-treatment
neutral detergent such as washing-up liquid or Stergene
white vinegar

★★**Glycerine**. Available at chemists, glycerine is used to soften and dissolve hardened stains. Particularly helpful on wool and other water-sensitive fabrics.

★★**Pet stain remover**. Specially formulated to clean and deodorise pet stains. Look for Bissell 'Not on the Carpet' Accident Cleaner, or Shaws No-Stain, from pet shops, hardware shops and department stores.

★★**Petroleum jelly**. White petrolatum, such as Vaseline. Used to soften and break up hardened grease and oil stains.

★★**Soap**. When stain removal procedures call for soap, use a mild, pure soap such as Fairy. Bar soap such as Lux is okay, but for stain removal don't use bar soaps that contain colouring, skin conditioners, or deodorants. And don't use soap on stains unless the instructions specifically tell you to—it sets some stains, such as fruit!

★**Acetone**. A special solvent helpful in removing paint, nail polish, model glue and lacquer. Available at paint stores, hobby shops and chemists. Never use acetone on acetate, triacetate, or modacrylic, or you'll end up with some extra buttonholes—acetone melts and dissolves fabrics like these. Use it with care on rayon, silk, or wool. It should be safe for most other fabrics, but always pre-test to be sure. Acetone is very flammable and gives off **poisonous** fumes, so always work with it in a well-ventilated place and never around sparks or flame. Protect your work surface, too, because it can damage furniture finishes and plastics. Nail polish remover (non-oily) is a good alternative.

Excellent Additions to Any Stain Kit

spotting brush
nylon scrubbing pad
absorber such as cat litter
methylated or surgical spirit
colour remover
glycerine
stain remover
petroleum jelly
soap such as Fairy
a medium-stiff brush for dry brushing
distilled water, if you have very hard water

★**Amyl Acetate.** Can safely remove nail polish, lacquer, and model glue from acetates and other fabrics that would be damaged by acetone. Buy the chemically pure kind, available at chemists. Protect your work surface when using it, because it too can **damage furniture finishes and plastics**. Again, non-oily nail polish remover is a good alternative.

★**Mangers De-Solv-it.** A citrus oil product especially good for dissolving adhesives and gum. Sold in supermarkets and hardware stores. Must be removed by laundering after use to avoid leaving an oil stain.

★**Proprietary grease solvents.** These products are widely available and come in liquid and aerosol formulations. When buying aerosols, look for products which do not contain chlorofluorocarbons (CFCs) and are 'ozone friendly'. Examples of grease solvents include Dabitoff, Beaucaire, The Stain Slayer, Stain Devils, K2r Stain Remover Spray. Always follow the manufacturer's instructions carefully when using these products. Keep them away from flame (don't smoke when you use them); use in a well-ventilated room and make sure you inhale as little of the vapour as possible.

Make sure you read the section on Safety (p. 64–66) before you use _any_ chemical stain remover.

---

5 The ABCs of Stainbusting

The Tricks of the Trade

If I told you tennis, photography, playing the piano, or something else you really wanted to learn had forty or fifty basic principles involved, you'd flinch, but you would probably still tackle them. Well, stain removal really has only three, and you can learn them just by watching. You can pull up a chair in front of any washing machine and watch—and you'll know all the basics of clever, efficient spot removal.

Chemical action is the soap, solvent, or other chemical we use to cut the smut—to dissolve the stain stuff and get it in solution (floating in the water). It's the detergent, in the case of our friend the washing machine.

Mechanical action is the movement involved: blotting, brushing, scraping or agitation—a special technique you'll learn for stainbusting—that helps the chemicals to do their job. It breaks up and removes the bulk of the mess so they **can** do it. And it helps work the chemicals in so they can perform faster and better. In your washing machine, it's the agitator.

Flushing or rinsing with water or solvent then carries the stain stuff away just like a silt-laden stream spirits off our topsoil.

Yes...spot and stain removal is that simple!

And you can make it even simpler by practising the well-known technique of executive management: delegation. You can use your nous to get your washing machine to do most of the work. Feed the washing machine most of your problems and with a bit of timing and prudence, it will get three of every four stains out of your life.

The specialised stainbusting techniques that follow come into play when you're working on dry-cleanable garments, delicate washables, carpet, upholstery, and other items you can't machine wash, and for stains that don't respond to laundering. It's always a good idea to launder washable items after the stain removal

process is finished to make sure the spotting chemicals are completely removed.

The Basic Stainbusting Techniques

Blot. Liquids just love to find a dry place, so help them along. Blotting is simply applying absorbent material which will slurp up the stain—blotting a spill while it's still wet is a hundred times more effective than trying to force it out after it's dry. Good, quick blotting will take care of a lot of spills—and if *you* don't soak 'em up, believe me, whatever they're spilled on will, and then you'll pay the price to get them out!

For fresh liquid spills, blotting is usually the first step to remove as much liquid as possible before applying any kind of stain remover. On carpets and upholstery, where flushing and rinsing are impossible, blotting comes into play again. We apply a chemical, let it work, and then blot it out again. Unless otherwise

50

specified, always blot with a clean white cotton cloth (see p. 41).

When finishing carpet stain removal, it's always a good idea to blot to prevent stains from doing their magical reappearing act (see p. 103).

Scrape. Scraping spots always makes me think of that crafty rubber spatula someone invented to scrape the cake mixture out of the bowl so there was nothing left for us children to lick up. A flat surface like this used gently can indeed scoop up every bit of a substance. In spot removal, scraping is used both to remove loose material from the surface and to work chemical spotters into a stain. For either operation, the scraper should be held fairly flat against the surface and worked back and forth **gently** with a sliding motion. Don't use the edge or point of the scraper to 'dig' or gouge a stain—this will amost certainly damage the fabric. Use special care when scraping delicate or loosely woven fabrics, or acetate, which marks easily. Be patient, and use light pressure, sliding the scraper back and forth gently to break up crusty stains, and to work the spotter into the fabric. As the spotter loosens the stain, the scraper removes the softened material, opening up the next layer to the action of the chemical.

Dry-brush. This is the only brushing to do in stain removal: a light brushing with a medium-stiff brush to get rid of dry, caked-on spots such as mud. Remember that you want to knock it loose,

not scrub it deeper into the fibre, so use a gentle lifting motion to flick the particles up and away from the surface, and use a vacuum to get the rest. Fine powders such as flour, face powder, or photocopier toner should always be vacuumed.

Always dry-brush and vacuum before working on a dry carpet or upholstery stain, to break loose and remove as much dry soil as you can. You can also dry-brush to remove powdered spot removers such as K2r, or dried poultices (see p. 57). The only way to use a brush during the 'wet' part of spotting is tamping or light pounding to agitate the fibres (see p. 55), never to scrub. Scrubbing a spot only causes it to spread and you 'fur' the fibres, so before you know it your carpet or cardigan has an Afro.

Freeze. A man in Alaska (it was 68 below that morning) once hit his spare tyre with a hammer and it shattered. That gives you an idea of freeze power, and it's by far the best way to remove gobs of gum, tar, candle wax, which only get messier when softened with a solvent.

If you use ordinary ice cubes on a water-sensitive fabric, put them in a well-sealed plastic bag. Small gummed-up items can just be popped into the freezer. Once the gum has frozen hard, immediately (before it has a chance to warm up and soften again) give it a few good whacks with the handle of your butter knife to fracture the brittle mass. Quickly scrape back and forth to break it up further into crumbs and make them 'powder' off. Then brush or vacuum away the crumbs quickly, or they'll re-adhere as soon as they soften.

Most spots of this type are in carpeting, which will tolerate a fairly heavy-handed attack if you make sure the knife blade is blunt and smooth, with no nicks or serrations to catch fibres. On a delicate fabric, pluck and scrape the crumbs away with your fingernail.

Soak. Like your washing machine, soaking can do a lot of the work for you, and soaking is free! Soaking was the rule for any rusted or stubborn machine parts on the farm where I grew up. Instead of attacking the item with chisels and hammers, instead of beating or poking it to death, we sprayed it with a solvent and left it. After the solvent had worked on the rust for a while, the offending part would almost fall off by itself.

Patience is a virtue in many things, but especially in stain removal. A chemical or liquid often needs to sit on the surface for a while to penetrate and soften a stain. Soak for at least 30

After You Drop It

You were intrigued by another customer's food selection and crash! You push your tray off the self-service counter, and everyone gets a close look at what *you* picked as it dynamically displays itself all over the floor. Biscuits roll 20 feet away and come to rest under the most beautiful person's chair. The drink splashes three feet up the legs of the nearby table and all over the next customer in the queue. The peas bounce everywhere, sprinkling the cafeteria offerings colourfully, but not nearly as colourfully as your fall, which shot barbecued pork all the way down the queue.

It's unquestionably one of life's most embarrassing moments. You've done it in supermarkets too, pulled a bottle off the shelf and watched it crash to the floor—and you've knocked over your cup or glass at the table any number of times. I once tried to cut frozen butter; it squirted like a torpedo across the living-room carpet at an elegant dinner.

Accidents like this are like a public announcement: 'Look at that idiot' and our face is not just red but stained with what we fell on.

It's bound to happen again, so remember, onlookers always feel more uncomfortable than you do. The minute you take control of the spill, you've won! Take full responsibility for it, and you'll have everyone on your side.

Act quickly and even dramatise a bit if necessary to keep the mess from hurting anyone or anything. Come up with a joke: 'Last time I spilled it on my boss's lap.' Quickly take out a credit card and scoop and scrape the remains on to the tray or plate. You'll be amazed how fast and easy it is, and it'll impress the crowd so much they'll probably applaud you. Lay napkins in the liquid to absorb it quickly. Your ineptitude turns into an opportunity to be congratulated, and you might even get a free meal out of it! Never run—things like broken glass could cause problems injurious to far more than pride. Just be careful cleaning the stuff off people's legs or laps— black eyes don't match red faces!

minutes, and longer periods (up to overnight for sturdy fabrics) will often be more effective. Don't overdo it with coloured fabrics, though—some dyes run when soaked for too long.

When the directions call for a washable item to be soaked, just immerse it (or the stained part) in a bowl filled with the solution. Soak dry-cleanables, carpet, and upholstery by folding a clean white cotton cloth into a pad, dampening it with the solution,

Look Out!—It's All About...

Our new house was almost finished, and we moved in just hours before my wife and newest daughter Cindy were due home from the hospital. Picking-up time came and I still hadn't hung the double doors on the side entrance. I decided I could do that later, so I left and brought mother and the new baby home. But one hour was long enough for the biggest cow in the herd to walk into the middle of the living room and drop the most enormous cow-pat you can imagine.

I cleaned it off the newly laid cork tile floor quickly, but it wasn't until much later, when I was reading, painting, dusting and moving that I realised that that great green stain wasn't the whole story. As time went by I found splatters on the wall, on the library books, under the piano, on top of pictures, even on the pencil sharpener.

Let that be a lesson to you about stains. We get so distracted by the main stain that often we don't realise in hit our collar, tie, shirt and belt before it came to rest on our thigh.

Stains get around—they bounce, seep, splash, run and hide, even in the very thing you're cleaning. Never assume that the big one is the only one! Stop, and look around. The mechanic doesn't just repair what you tell him about, he checks the rest of the car too, just in case!

and applying it to the stained area. Don't use too big a pad or get it too wet—the liquid should be confined to the area of the stain, not spread all over the surface. You may have to re-dampen the pad occasionally to prevent it from drying out.

Sponge. Sponge may be what our worthless brother-in-law does, who manages to get a loan out of everybody, but it's also the most useful technique of applying spotter to stains. Put down a pad of folded, clean white absorbent cloth and lay the stained article on it, face down if possible. Use another clean cloth pad to apply the spotting chemical to the back of the stain. Work from the outside of the stain toward the centre to avoid spreading it, and keep the damp area as small as possible by using short, light strokes and the bare minimum of liquid.

Use the cloth pad like a sponge to 'push' the spotting solution through the fabric, and as you work the spotter through, change the pad underneath as necessary to keep it dry and clean enough to check for colour (stain or dye) transfer. Keep on sponging until no more colour is being transferred. Change the sponging pad, too, as it picks up colour, to prevent it spreading the stain.

Tamp. The professional term for the right way to use a spotting brush, which is never to rub or scrub, but to **agitate** the stain.

As I said earlier, some kind of physical action is usually needed to help dislodge the soil from a surface so it can be removed. But instead of dragging a brush across the surface as we do in scrubbing (not all that effective, as well as risking damage to delicate surfaces), tamping 'agitates'—jiggles and jostles—just the area of the stain itself, to help break all the stain matter free. To tamp, spread the stained fabric out face up on a hard, smooth, level surface like a piece of glass or the top of the washing machine. Strike the stain lightly but squarely with the flat face of a spotting brush (see p. 42 for details.) Be careful not to hit with the hard corner of the brush or the edge of the bristles—this will distort or damage the fabric. Use only as much force as the fabric will tolerate. Tightly woven, durable fabrics and carpeting can withstand fairly forceful tamping, while loosely woven or delicate fabrics call for a gentler touch. You're not trying to beat it to death, just to strike hard enough with the ends of the bristles to break up the crust of the stain and work the spotting agent into it. Even if the instructions don't specifically call for it, you can tamp whenever you need to, to loosen residue or help the spotter to penetrate.

Flush. Flushing means applying liquid so lavishly that it flows through the fabric and washes out whatever it is you're trying to remove—the stain itself or the spotting chemical you've already used. Flushing can be done with an squeeze bottle, spray bottle, or even an eyedropper. Flush from the back of the fabric whenever possible, so the stain is washed out the way it came in, instead of being forced through the fabric. Put an absorbent cloth pad on the face of the spot, and apply the liquid through the back no faster than the pad can absorb it, to avoid enlarging the wet area. Change the pad as needed.

On carpets and upholstery, flush by sponging the liquid on and blotting it out with a clean towel.

For some stains, as indicated under the individual stain removal instructions, flush by running water rapidly through the fabric under a tap, or pouring boiling water through it to flush out stains such as red fruit juice.

Bleach. Using bleach is like hiring a hit man after all peaceful persuasive methods have failed. When you've done everything you know how to do and there's still a stain, you may want to resort to bleaching. This isn't a step to be taken lightly, because bleaching can damage whatever you're working on, as well as alter the colour. If it's a choice between bleaching it and binning it, that's easy, but be sure to exhaust all the alternatives. See p. 29 for a breakdown of the various bleaches available, what they can be used on and safety precautions.

It's always a good idea to test any bleach on a hidden area, especially if you're not sure what kind of fabric you're working with. Whenever possible, bleach the whole object, not just the stained area—if something loses a little bit of colour all over, it'll be a lot less noticeable than a single light spot. (When you're spot-bleaching, things tend to look pretty good until the item dries.) Be especially wary of spot-bleaching dry-cleanables. Wetting the fabric before you apply bleach will make it work better. Always rinse bleach out as soon as you reach the colour you want, and rinse well in between if changing types of bleach. Be sure to follow label directions to protect yourself and your possessions, and never use a stronger bleach than necessary to do the job.

Apply a poultice. A poultice (a paste made by mixing a powdered cleaning chemical with water or solvent) will pull certain types of stains out of porous materials. A paste made of a bleaching cleanser such as Vim, Ajax or Jif, plus water or lemon juice will often coax stains out of Formica worktops, for instance. Just cover the stain with the poultice and let it dry, then wipe away the powder after it dries. Specialised stone cleaning poultices are available for dealing with stains in marble, terrazzo, and other

---

Residue... Will Never Do

Remember when Mother told you about iron in spinach, or germs on your grazed knee? You looked good and hard and never saw either, so you just took it on trust and ate the spinach and bore the disinfectant's sting as it killed the germs. Time for some more trust in what I'm going to tell you.

When a stain or spot is gone—when it seems to your very own eye that it's totally out, gone, not a trace left—there may still be something in there. Even though you can't see it, some of the cleaner, solvent, or soap that removed the stain may have remained in the fabric or on the surface. Professionals call this detergent residue, and if you don't get all of it out, although it's invisible now, it will: stiffen the spot, collect soil, create its own stain—and even make some fabrics deteriorate.

This residue isn't hard to get out, and it's generally done with a rinsing agent. For alkaline spotters we sometimes use vinegar, a very mild acid. Most times, we use a good, thorough water rinse. This is one reason why the final rinse step is so important, especially in carpet. Don't forget to do it.

Catch It Quick, Before It Can Stick...

★ Liquid spills. Blot up as much as you can and sponge the spot with water before it dries.

★ Dry, powdery stains (toner, mud, etc). Vacuum or dry-brush to remove all you can before applying any kind of liquid.

★ Dry, crusty deposits. Scrape, then soak if needed to loosen stubborn stuck-on stuff.

★ Oily or greasy stains. Use absorbent material to suck up as much oil as possible before wetting the spot with solvent.

★ Gum, tar, and other sticky stuff. Freeze, shatter, and scrape to remove the bulk of it before applying solvent.

★ Penetrating stains (in stone, concrete, brick). Use a poultice to draw the stain matter out.

---

porous masonry finishes. K2r, the aerosol solvent spotter often so effective in removing oily or greasy stains from wallpaper, stone, and raw wood, is actually a poultice of solvents and absorbents.
Rinse. Rinse either between steps in stain removal, or as you finish the whole process, to get all the spotting chemicals out. Most wet stain removal procedures end with rinsing. I use 'rinse' in this book, almost exclusively to mean 'rinse with water.' For washables, this can mean holding a garment under the tap or dipping it repeatedly into a sink or basin of water. When you can't do this, as with dry-cleanables, you'll have to resort to what's called 'sponge-rinsing.' This means sponging water through the spot using a clean cloth pad, keeping the wet area small and using an absorbent pad underneath to soak up the water. Always feather the edges as you finish. For carpet and upholstery, sponge-rinsing means sponging on clear water and then blotting it out again, taking care not to use more water than necessary.

Rinsing isn't an optional step—if you skip the rinse you risk reactions between chemicals that aren't supposed to be there at the same time, and damage done by chemical residues left behind in carpet or clothing. Unrinsed residues will also attract dirt like a magnet to a freshly cleaned spot.

Air dry means turning to nature—fresh air with perhaps a sprinkling of sun and breeze but no motors or heaters, additives, or preservatives. Air drying is the safe way to get the water out,

so that you can get a closer look at your stainbusting results. When you've laundered or spotted something stained, always air dry it so any stains that might still be lurking unnoticed aren't set hard.

Feather. We've all removed a spill from something that's slightly dirty all over, only to end up with a highly noticeable 'clean spot' that looks worse than the stain! Many stain removers, including water, will also leave a ring when they dry, especially if the spot is allowed to dry in the centre first, leaving a wet outer ring. To avoid this happening, always 'feather' or blend the edges as you finish a stain removal operation.

When you *apply* solvent or water to a stain, work from the outside in towards the centre, to keep the stain from spreading. **Keep the wet area as small as possible**. Then, when you rinse, especially in the final rinse, work from the centre back towards the outside, and blend the wet area into the dry area beyond with light, lifting, outward strokes. Instead of a distinct line between a wet spot and dry surrounding fabric, you want a graduated dampness from wet, to damp, to almost dry.

59

You can also feather by blotting the dampened area as dry as possible between two clean dry cloths, then drying the spot quickly with brisk strokes from a clean towel. Or you can use a hair dryer, starting at the outside and working in towards the middle. The trick is to make sure the spot dries from the edges in towards the middle.

Never forget to feather as you finish removing stains from dry cleanables and upholstery fabrics.

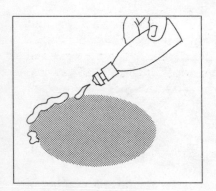
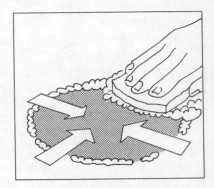
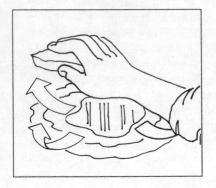
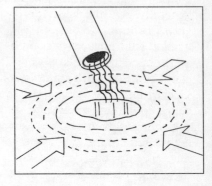

6 The Rogue's Gallery of Stains

From Easy to Impossible

Spots and spills happen every day, and many of them don't deserve a second thought. You drizzle a few drops of diet cola down your T-shirt, or the dog jumps up and puts muddy prints on a child's jeans. Most minor incidents like these come out in the wash and are never heard of again. It's the minority, that little 10 per cent of stains, that cause 90 per cent of stain headaches. And most of these real baddies crop up in the course of everyday activities like putting on make-up, polishing shoes, painting the living room, cleaning the oven, or trying to improve the health of houseplants. Here's a rundown on the range of stain villains, from the small-time crooks to the serious repeat offenders.

Water-soluble stains. This gang contains the largest number of common stains, but they're also the easiest to get rid of and they generally give the least trouble. Some are real pushovers. This group includes any staining substance (such as coffee, tea, soft drinks, fruit juice, water-soluble ink, wine) that can be dissolved and removed with water or water-based cleaners. Many of these stains come out with a simple wash, if the stained item is washable.

Greasy and oily stains. The second largest bunch, these are the stains containing grease, fat, or oil, and it usually takes a grease-dissolving solvent or water-soluble degrease to remove them completely. Stains in this category include lubricating greases and oils, cooking oils, animal fat, and oily foods. Engine oil, salad dressing, bacon grease, butter, and chip spots are common examples. Some of these will come out of the washables with the aid of a laundry pre-treatment. On dry-cleanable items, and for heavy grease stains on washables, petroleum solvent is often needed to break down the oil.

Combination stains. These are tough guys: they're the spots that have both greasy and non-greasy ingredients, and require a multi-method attack to remove. Coffee with cream, gravy, creamy salad

dressings, and chocolate are all examples of stains that contain oils, greases, and fats, along with starches, sugars, tannin, and other water-soluble stuff. A common mistake here is to remove the worst of it (the water-soluble part), and ignore the oily part. It may look all right until the oil darkens with age or heat to leave a permanent stain.

Dye stains. Now we're getting to the real baddies. There are many stains in which the staining agent is a colourant or dye. Dyes are used in everything from antibiotics to aftershaves to after-dinner drinks; sandals to suntan lotion to the Sunday papers. And some of them bond to fabrics so tightly they're impossible to remove. But many will come out if you persevere. The rule on dye stains is: don't give up too soon. They're rough customers, but they can often be rehabilitated. If you have a tough dye stain like red wine, or ink try, try and try again—persistence often pays off.

Chemical stains. These are the hardened felons and there's not much hope for them. When you're hit by one of these, look out! In chemical stains a chemical alters or destroys the dye in a fabric or surface—or the fabric or surface itself—leaving a permanently bleached, discoloured, or damaged spot. More or less all you can do is replace that section of the material (such as put a plug in

62

carpet), or put a lace mat or rug over the spot. It's hard to believe how many common household products contain chemicals that can injure or deface carpet, upholstery, furniture, and clothes, and how unaware we are of their existence. Since stains of this type are so deadly, let's take a closer look at the most likely suspects:

Acids and alkalis. The strong acids found in many lavatory cleaners, tile cleaners, corn and callous removers, and even in vomit and urine can cause colour changes in carpet and upholstery fabrics. Strong alkalis, such as the caustic soda found in many drain cleaners and oven cleaners, will not only devastate the dye, but often the fabric itself.

Bleaches. We all know that liquid chlorine bleach will leave a lightened or bleached spot if spilled on the carpet or spattered on clothes. But most people don't realise that mildew removers and even the milder laundry bleaches trodden into the carpet can also cause dye changes if left on for long enough.

Other chemical baddies. Some liquid plant foods and fertilisers bleach out carpet dye, in case you ever wondered what those dull yellow spots were under pots and planters. Some pesticides can also discolour carpet.

That's the stain gang, from least to worst.

7 Stain Safety

Playing It Safe for You and the Surface

When removing stains, substances that can burn, splash, dissolve or create fumes are often used, so there is a lot to watch out for, to make sure you live to enjoy your brilliant removal job. A dry cleaner once refused to clean my sleeping bag the day before a big camping trip. He explained that the toxic fumes from the dry cleaning solvent remain in the bag for some time afterwards, and if you tuck your head inside to escape the gnats, it could be your last camping trip! An upholstery cleaner told me about a chair that was cleaned using flammable solvent spotters. The fabric seemed to dry, so the owner sat down and lit a cigarette—and the whole thing went up in smoke. Cats, too, have curled their little whiskered faces into solvent-shampooed sofas and been put to sleep permanently by the lingering vapours. Many of the chemicals used in stain removal can be dangerous if not handled properly. Don't panic and think living with a stain might be better than losing life or limb. But do follow these safety guidelines to keep out of trouble.

First... Protect Yourself!

★ Always work in a well-ventilated area, since many chemicals give off hazardous fumes. Expectant mothers should be especially careful. Well-ventilated means fresh air flowing in and 'bad' air flowing out—a room with windows open at both ends, or with a fan going. Or outside on the patio, etc. Don't inhale the fumes any more than is unavoidable.

★ Never smoke or work around flame or sparks when using flammable solvents (alcohol, methylated or surgical spirit, amyl acetate, acetone). And you don't just get sparks from rubbing sticks together—sparks are created by light switches, the automatic starters in central heating boilers and many kinds of heaters, and even static electricity. So don't think this caution doesn't really apply to you.

★ Put oil or solvent-soaked rags in a metal container when you're finished with them because they can catch fire spontaneously. (Yes, that means without any help from anybody.) And don't dry rags used for solvent in a tumble dryer.

★ Don't even **think** of mixing two or three chemicals together so you can do several stain removal steps in one fell swoop. Mix spotting chemicals only according to directions—some chemicals create toxic gases when combined (and mixed chemicals will kill you a lot faster than mixed drinks).

* Buy and store only small amounts of stain removers. Some substances break down during long storage and should not be used.

* Remember, many chemicals are **poisonous**. Never decant them into another bottle without labelling clearly.

* Store all dangerous chemicals up high or locked away out of the reach of children—and make sure they have tight lids and clear labels.

* Strong acids, caustics, and solvents call for rubber gloves, not bare hands.

* Don't switch containers. It doesn't take long to forget what's in what, and some chemicals react with certain container materials. And even if you do write the new contents on the bottle, most people seem to go by the colour and shape of the container, especially when they're in a hurry.

Second... Protect What You're Working On

* Identify the stain **and** the fabric before applying any chemical. Using the wrong stuff can set the stain or cause irreparable colour loss and fabric damage.

* Take the time to think, look carefully, and read the label again.

* Work in good light, so you can see the stains and spots and the action.

* Stay cool. Heat from hot water washing, drying, or ironing can set many stains.

* Be patient. A little waiting (for the chemical to work) often accomplishes more than a lot of scraping and scrubbing.

* Be gentle. Rubbing, squeezing, and beating with rocks only forces stains further in and can destroy more delicate fabrics. Heavy-handed spotting technique can distort, bruise, and fray fibres, leaving an ugly spot even if the stain comes out.

* Finish! Always flush or rinse out the spotting chemical when you've finished with a spot, and don't skip the in-between steps called for in the instructions. Flush out one stain remover before applying another. This eliminates bad reactions. Letting chemicals mix or dry out in the fabric can be damaging.

* Follow label directions for mixing, storing, and using spotting chemicals. Used too strong or in the wrong order, some of them can weaken, fade, or even eat a hole in the very item you're trying to salvage.

8 Working With Your Dry Cleaner

When to Go to the Pros

Deep down I'm a do-it-yourselfer. Doing it yourself is unbeatable . . . if you **can** do it yourself!

But we've all spent an hour and £5 worth of chemicals on a stain (and still not got rid of it) when we could have taken it to a pro for £3.50.

I'm not talking about coin-op dry cleaning, either. Signs that say, 'Do your own dry cleaning for £1 a pound' only tell you that you're on your own with what comes out—and bad spots and stains generally don't. If the solvent bath doesn't dissolve the stain, it'll still be there, only more visible, when your ballgown or bedspread emerges!

It may cost a little more, but what a dry cleaner makes isn't all profit. Whether you or they do the job, it still involves quite a bit of time to work on the stain, and often quite a bit of material. For £5-6 a few times a year, I'd take all the really troublesome items to the cleaners.

They're professionals! They want everything to turn out perfect. So choose a favourite and stick with them. The more you work with them, the more they'll work with and for you.

Professional cleaners have chemicals most of us don't have access to. They're highly effective, but also highly dangerous, and take expert training to use. The pros also have special tools like steam guns and a lot more of that irreplaceable experience than you or I. They face problem stains every day, and on every imaginable surface.

They're your friends, but they're not magicians or faith healers. They can't restore lost colour or serious damage, or grow new hair on worn velvet or moth-eaten fur coats. They're also not mind readers. They don't automatically know what's on something, or what you did to the stain before you brought it in to them. Never cut off tags or labels (even if **you** have memorised them), and that includes labels on curtains, bedding, upholstery, hats, etc.

What else would dry cleaners say about how you can help them do a dazzling job?

★ Let me do it all. Don't wash or dry or iron in stains before you bring them in.

★ Let me do your wools, crepes, silks, taffeta or any questionable piece or fabric—I'll save you time and money.

★ Don't wait! If it needs professional help, now is better and cheaper than later.

★ Removing stains involves enough detective work already, so tell me, or attach a note to the item explaining where the stain is, what you think it might be and how long it's been there.

★ If the piece has a special problem—if something is damaged— tell me please, so we won't end up blaming each other.

★ Empty the pockets (**all** of them).

★ If you've tried some home remedy (for **any** stain removal steps)

68

already, be sure to tell me exactly what you did, and maybe I can salvage the situation.

★ Bring it in unravaged. Don't just say, 'Oh well, it's going to the cleaners anyway', and toss it on the floor, drag it around, bundle it up, or stuff it into a greasy car boot. More damage is often done on the way to the cleaners than was done originally.

★ Don't get your hopes up too high on anything decorated. Suede, fur or vinyl trim, velvet collars, anything with metallic threads, sequins, beadwork, appliques, iron-on transfers, tassels, or fringes are between hard and impossible to clean, never mind remove stains from.

★ Accept the fact, that I'll do the best I can, but there may be nothing anyone can do for it.

★ In case you've wondered why we say we have to clean the whole thing, not just try to remove the ten-year-old toffee from it: it's because *we* want to be sure all spotting chemicals are completely removed when we've finished, too.

9 Knowing When to Stop

The Truth About Certain Types of Stains

Many of my TV and radio interviews are phone-ins, and which subject always steals the show? You've guessed it—stains. The trouble is that for an alarming number of the questions I can't give a useful or truly restorative reply.

1. 'Mr Aslett, my bath has black stains in the bottom, and I've used bleach, powdered cleansers, acid, caustic soda and even sandpaper on it.' 'How old is your bath?' 'Forty-six years.'

2. 'Mr Aslett, I have this filthy 30-year-old carpet covered in stains from the dog I used to have. If I have it cleaned professionally what can I expect?'

3. (Believe it or not, I get asked this one a lot, too.) 'Mr Aslett, my husband smokes and there are cigarette burns on his armchair and the carpet around it—how can I clean them out?'

4. 'Don, my toddler scribbled on my living room walls with a permanent marker—what do I need to get it off?'

5. Mr Aslett, my uncle has a favourite leather jacket he wears for working on the farm. It's stiff and stained from 25 years of fence mending, and muck spreading—how do I clean it?'

These questions, encouraged by the host who claims I know everything about cleaning, come one after the other and there's only one answer (and it's all bad news)—the coat is headed for the last knacker's yard, the ink has penetrated not only the paint but the bricks and mortar, and is now a permanent part of the decor. About all you can expect, madam, is a reasonably clean, worn-out carpet full of old pet stains. That carpet was dead 10 years ago, and even if you could remove aged, set urine stains it wouldn't grow the pile back! And, sir, that bath is too far gone, get rid of it. The 'stain' in the bottom is the cast iron showing through, you've worn off—scrubbed and bleached off—the porcelain!

Perhaps when our most treasured possession is stained those

aren't the answers we want to hear, but soils will be soils and some of them on the wrong thing at the right time produce a combination that spells total disaster. Sometimes, in spite of your most dedicated efforts (and your A+ in Third Form chemistry), you come up against a stain you just can't beat. To save yourself from stain-removal stress, you'll know it's time to throw in the towel rather than use it when:

★ You have to take the curtains down carefully so they won't disintegrate before you get them to the cleaners.

★ It'll cost £3 to clean the strawberry pop stain off that 75p straw hat.

★ The stain is still there after four goes through the washing machine.

★ You're wondering how this stain will go with the six others already on there.

★ You've bleached the trousers so many times they no longer match the jacket.

★ The stain is the best-looking part of it.

That's not a stain, it's *damage*. This includes:

★ Anything badly scorched. Light scorch marks from ironing can often be removed, but a heavy scorch is actual fibre damage, and won't come out.

★ Anything burned—which means melted fibres and a charred surface even if there isn't an actual hole.

★ Anything badly frayed. Shirt collars and cuffs abraded by whiskers and bracelets for example, will look dirty or stained even when they're clean, because the frizzed fabric reflects light differently.

★ Anything you've scrubbed or scoured to death. Once you've scored the smooth surface of your satin blouse, lacerated the lace tablecloth, or rubbed a bald spot in a velour armrest trying to remove a stain, it's never going to look the same—face it.

★ Part of the surface or material is gone—removed, destroyed, sanded, eaten away. (Moth holes and battery acid burns, for example, will still be there after all your efforts.) If you have a dropped-frying-pan burn in front of the cooker, get a professional to plug in a new piece of flooring and stop blaming yourself because you can't get it out with lemon juice and baking soda.

The stain is purely and simply *permanent*. Some stains just don't come out. Indelible inks, permanent markers, red food dyes, some medicines, and other dye-type stains sometimes become a part of the fabric. To get them out, you'd have to strip **all** the dye out, and then you'd be left with a light spot. Dye changes can be irreversible, too. Many common household products can alter or bleach dyes, leaving a permanent faded spot (see p. 62). The alcohol in cologne, perfume, and drinks can cause dyes to bleed and run in some fabrics, making a stain that can't be repaired. Even water will cause dye to run in some silks. And easily removed stains such as coffee, sugar, mustard, or blood can be set by heat, alkali, or acids, to the point where they become permanent. Sometimes a professional spotter can remove stains you can't cope with, but even the pros run across stains that just won't cooperate. They just mark them 'permanent' and forget about them. That's what you should do, too.

Sometimes it just isn't worth it. If the nail polish puddle is in the middle of the living room carpet, you'll probably want to do whatever you have to to get it out. But if it's on a cheap white acetate blouse, you'll spend more than that in time, chemicals, and energy trying to remove it, and the blouse will probably never be the same anyway. Better to chalk it up to experience and buy a new one. Instead of spending half of Saturday trying to get the shoe polish off the hem of an ancient pair of white trousers, why not de-mote them to painting gear and go out instead? Some stains, even if ultimately removable, just don't deserve the effort and expense needed to get them out.

I know it takes a lot of guts to redefine your Pringle cashmere as a gardening jumper, and a lot of money to reupholster, or change a worktop. I've seen some of you diehards spend hours trying to pick all the paint specks off a worn and faded chair cover. More power to your persistence, especially if stain removal is your hobby. Just remember that because it's your best or your favourite, or unspeakably sentimental doesn't make it immune to permanent damage. We all have to go sometime and it's not clever to waste too much time trying to pull off a miracle—the smart spotter knows when to say when.

Stain-Salvaging Strategies, or Creative Concealment

When we come up against stains that won't shift, there's still an alternative. It's called 'creative concealment'—whimsical (and even some practical) things you can do with an impossible stain in an unditchable object. After all, stain injury is mostly cosmetic—the object in question is usually still functional.

★ The 'add an alligator approach'—sew an attractive applique or monogram or a pretty patch over it.

★ Embroider over it.

★ Add a new button or pocket, or a decorative edging.

★ Decorate it (reverse psychology approach)—add beads or sequins or a couple of complementary colours to it, outline it in black or silver.

★ Cut it out and hem the edges (if you dare).

★ Dye the whole thing darker, or that colour, or dip the whole thing in the stain.

★ Bleach the whole thing, or parts of it (tie-dye returns!).

★ Repeat the stain at regular intervals.

★ Turn it inside out, upside down, or wear it backwards.

★ Restyle/remodel it. Convert it to a one-piece or a two-piece (you probably never liked the jacket anyway).

★ Depending on where the stain is on your clothing or curtain, you could add a belt or a tieback.

★ Amputate it—cut off the sleeves or legs, shorten the skirt, or carve, sand, or whittle it away.

★ Wear a corsage, badge, or big necklace over it, or a wide tie, scarf or shawl.

★ Hold your arm/briefcase, or shoulder bag over it, or comb your hair over it.
★ Place a rug, footstool, or potted plant over it, or hang a picture or poster over it.
★ Get a new piece patched in or have it rewoven.
★ Disguise it by blending in the edges (with wax crayon or permanent markers, for instance).
★ Paint, carpet, or texture the whole thing (after sealing the stain, in the case of painting).
★ Hide the whole thing (if it belongs to somebody else).
★ Give it to the jumble sale.
★ Save it to make a Guy Fawkes on 5 November.
★ Bury it with the body.
★ Cut it up for a patchwork quilt.
★ Reduce it to paint rags.
★ Recycle it.
★ Use it to fill a crack somewhere.
★ Snip off a little piece of it to save for sentiment and get **rid** of the rest!

10 Prevent Those Stains

It's a Lot Easier Than Removing Them

Have you ever met one of those people who can get more done alone than five of the rest of us put together? They don't seem to move any faster, work any harder, have any mysterious machine, they just get plenty-plus accomplished every single day, at work and at home. Do you want to know their secret? It will not only solve 80 per cent of your spot and stain stumpers, but a lot of your other life problems as well. My father was one of those miracle producers, and one day I finally realised how he did it.

Dad made a new livestock trailer, a beautiful blue contraption we pulled behind the truck. When we returned from our first trip with it, every side of the trailer was splattered, plastered, coated with mud, tar, even gravel flung up by the tyres. It took me two hours to clean it off and the trailer never looked quite as snazzy afterwards. 'I knew I should have taken the time to put mud flaps on it!' Dad announced. 'Mud flaps?' I said. Dad quickly cut two pieces of rubber and tucked one in behind each tyre. It only took a few minutes and forever after, all we ever had on the trailer was a bit of easily removed dust. That single device saved two to three hundred hours of cleaning in a lifetime! My Dad did the same with everything on the farm. He installed splash guards, bumper guards, oil finishes, haystack covers, and even a system in animal pens to prevent manure spots, chewing, rubbing, and pawing. Dad's secret in life managment was that he didn't spend all his time repairing, restoring, cleaning up after, or de-spotting: he *prevented* the problem. That's not only a clever and cheap way to live, it's a lot easier on our surroundings and possessions.

Getting a stain out isn't as much of an accomplishment as you might think, because when you've finished (even if you've done a good job) you're only back where you started. You haven't gained any ground. So why are we so often taught to solve

problems instead of preventing them? Ninety per cent of the ads we see are for cures rather than preventatives. We can't wrap ourselves and everything we own in plastic, but we certainly can take advantage of some anti-stain strategies. Bibs are a beautiful example. Wise women use them, but new fathers seldom seem to understand that one minute spent bibbing baby saves who knows how long swabbing, finding clean clothes, changing, and coddling later—not to mention laundry time.

People are amazed that my company cleans a commercial building in six hours, when the previous contractor took twice as long each night to do it. It's not magic, just prevention. We install good doormats, more and better rubbish bins, educate the tenants, control building use and traffic, banish spotmakers, and guess what? It helps to eliminate work and damage. If we all found ways to prevent spots and stains at home, we'd not only be able to do without this and at least two dozen other books and pamphlets on stain removal, but thousands of gallons of cleaning chemicals, millions of hours of effort, and millions of pounds of costs. Successfully removing every spot may be wishful thinking, but preventing some of them in the first place isn't.

The mother who spreads a specially made mat under her baby's high chair knows two important principles of prevention:
1. Messes are going to happen—they're part of living.
2. Spreading the mat takes only fifteen seconds, but it'll take fifteen minutes to remove strained beetroot from the carpet—if we can do it.

We'll never totally eliminate spots and spills, but we can do a lot to keep them from becoming stains. It's better to know how to keep it out than how to get it out after it happens. Here are some excellent ways to do that.

The World's Greatest Stain and Spot Decoy—the Mat

So small, so unobtrusive, so inexpensive. Just lying there quietly, the right kind of door mat will stop thousands of spots and stains at the door, before they ever get in or on. It only takes one piece of cleaning equipment to clean a mat, and ten or more pieces to clean tar, mud, and animal mess out of the house once they get in.

The best mats on the market for this purpose are made from nylon carpeting with a nonslip rubber back for inside, and crisp grasslike polypropylene mats for outside, to knock off the 'big stuff' and withstand the weather for years. Just make sure they're at least four steps long, both inside and out.

Keep it Covered

I'm a good painter, and can usually brush and roll without slopping paint around. But I always put a cloth down, even for a ten-minute touch-up job. It takes a lot less time to throw a cover over the chair than it does to remove even a single paint spot from it. The ratio of time it takes to clean up, compared to cover up, is about fifty to one! It takes no more than three minutes to carefully spead a cloth over something you want to protect. Cleaning if off later is at least a two-hour job—if you can get it off, and if you can live with the bleached, scuffed, deglossed surface you end up with after the cleaning process.

Never use old newspapers, they just strain the stains and hide them until they settle in for good. They stick to your feet, and paints and liquids seep right through them. Another counterfeit cloth is the thin plastic type: hopeless. It sticks and clings to everything, and since it's transparent, holes and punctures are hard to see. So while you're enjoying the illusion all is well, the stain that sneaked through is firmly settling in for a long stay.

Dress for the Mess

You say you can't seem to win the stain war, because your job or situation involves eight straight hours of stain exposure like painting, pottery making, mud wrestling, gardening, working in fast food or on cars? No matter how careful you are, you just can't win? Then you need to be especially sure to dress yourself and your surroundings sensibly.

I always carry a set of overalls in my car, for instance, since you never know when you may break down or need to carry something, get on or under something, use grease, or change a tyre—and every one of these processes has amazing stain potential. If they get on your overalls that's okay—they're a badge of honour, even—but nice they aren't on the new Shetland sweater! If you or your work are stain prone, dress and design for it. Don't just say, 'I won't get any on me this time.'

The Napkin and the Hanky—Two Forgotten 'Bulletproof Vests' of Stain Control

These two handy little helpers can take the strain for many a stain, and be a big help both before and after. Don't leave home without them!

★ On your lap: they can catch it before it lands.
★ You can use them like a bib: to take the brunt of it, and a paper napkin certainly beats a silk tie.
★ They can blot and absorb spills.
★ They can be wrapped: around the sausage sandwich or ice

cream cone, so food fallout falls on them instead of on you.

★ They can serve as a washer/dryer combination: wet one end and dry with the other.

★ They make great containers for dangerous waste: to encase cores, peelings, not-quite-bare chicken bones, gum, and other gory details so they don't get a chance to stain.

★ They can even be a dam: to keep spills from flowing further.

Invisible Shields

In addition to obvious protectors like napkins and cover-up cloths many household surfaces and furnishings can be given an invisible protective shield against staining.

Soil retardants. Products like Scotchgard seal the pores of fabric and give the fibres a clear protective coating. Like a coat of varnish, it's unstainable and keeps stains and even moisture out. Stains don't penetrate, so they can just be wiped off the surface. Soil retardants not only keep liquid spills from sinking in, but make dry soil a lot easier to vacuum or brush out. The fabric releases all kinds of dirt much more easily because the soil is on the coating, not the fibre itself. Soil retardants are available for everything from carpet and upholstery to suits and ties. Many fabrics and carpets today are treated with retardant during manufacture, and these are well worth any extra cost.

Using retardant doesn't make anything stainproof for ever, though. With time and use retardant will wear off and need to be reapplied. And for maximum protection, it should be renewed every time you deep-clean treated carpet, clothing, or upholstery.

Masonry sealers. Masonry is a magnificent and maintenance-free material—but not if it's left bare and untreated. You shouldn't have any exposed concrete, brick, stone, or earth tile that isn't protected by a clear masonry seal—and that even includes the grout. It only takes one experience of removing smoke stains from an unsealed stone fireplace, or oil stains from a garage floor, to appreciate what sealers do. I sealed my fireplace 25 years ago and it still looks like new. You can get sealers that go on like varnish, leaving a smooth glossy film, or the penetrating kind that hardly alter the original appearance of the material. Sealers are available at DIY centres or anywhere that sells masonry or tiles. I like satin finish sealer for vertical surfaces and high gloss for floors. Outdoors, choose the kind designed for exterior use.

Wood finishes. Untreated or waxed wood floors, panelling, and furniture may look rich, but they're a poor way of protecting all-too-absorbent wood from stains, marks, rings, and smudges. You can get almost the same look with a coat of satin-finish polyurethane, and it'll keep stains out completely. A heatproof polyurethane varnish requires virtually no care and really speeds everyday dusting and cleaning.

Floor finishes. A layer of finish such as Bourneseal for cork or tiles, or Johnson's Klear for vinyl, helps floors resist staining. Black marks, for example, are a cinch to remove from a coat of wax. Even vinyl-coated floors can be made prettier—and kept from eventually growing dull—with a coat of floor finish.

Choose the Right Material

We set ourselves up for a lot of stains by the materials we surround ourselves with. Here are some of the most important to watch out for:

Carpet. The new stain-resistant carpet fibres, made mainly by Du Pont, are so much better at repelling stains than the older-generation yarns, it's silly to choose anything else—but some people still do.

Paint. Even the best brands of emulsion paint (no matter what the label says) aren't very scrubbable. They're more porous, harder to clean, and much more prone to staining than satin vinyl or satin wood finishes. If a matt look means that much to you, compromise and put on paint with satin or eggshell finish, which will stay spotless a lot longer.

Vinyl flooring. To outsmart stains, choose flooring with a clear vinyl wear layer on the top such as Rhino sheet vinyl, among many others. It's much more stain resistant than ordinary vinyl. And make sure it's sheet vinyl, not vinyl tile or anything with seams stains can seep down into.

Floor tiles. Forget about raw, unfinished quarry tiles, marble, slate, etc, or you'll be forever applying fresh sealer as foot traffic grinds and wears it away. You can get the same subtle look underfoot with satin glazed ceramic tile—and it's impervious to just about any stain. The protective finish is part of the tile, so it won't wear off. To head off the stain problems in the joints, get coloured grout reinforced with epoxy resin.

Clothing. Buy quality—stains comes out of better-made brands and fabrics more readily than from cheap and cheerful clothes. The more expensive garments often have built-in stain blockers—and even if they don't they usually repel stains better than bargain brands.

Bathroom fixtures. Vitreous china fixtures (even with white ones) are the best stain-fighters, with porcelain-coated cast iron coming a close second. Porcelain-coated steel is next best, followed by Corian and cultured marble. Shiny chrome is best for taps, from a stain-resisting standpoint.

Eliminate the Source

The class bully informed me one day (when I was still a five-stone weakling) that unless I stopped flirting with the prettiest girl in the class I was 'cruising for a bruising.' Likewise, a lot of your possessions are 'aiming for a staining.' Some of the major culprits you can eliminate without even missing them are:

Red food dye. Red is the worst colour for causing stains. Red-coloured pet foods can make for impossible vomit stains, so since Fido doesn't care whether or not his food looks 'meaty' (he's colour blind, after all) why not choose another colour? White wine is more versatile than red and leaves you with less of a stain, as well as less of a hangover. And white pasta sauces are less acid as well as more fashionable.

81

Markers. Most of the places where we use felt-tip markers don't actually need permanent ink, but we buy permanent ones anyway. When we end up ruining a dress shirt or tablecloth, we always wish we'd bought washable.

Medicines. Iodine was good in its day, but we have antiseptics now that do the job without ruining carpets and vanity tops. Some cough syrups and cold medications have enough red or yellow dye in them to colour Loch Ness. Our sinuses aren't impressed with the pretty colours, but our blankets or bathrobes may be— why take a chance?

Clothing. Fitness centres were clever enough to ban the wearing of black-soled shoes which mark the squash courts, but we continue to scuff floors at home with them. And the soles of 'mountain boots' not only black-mark floors, but constantly drip little gobs of mud or snow out of the cleats. And why have a leather jacket that constantly rubs dye on to your shirt collars; or a non-colourfast tracksuit that bleeds colour on to your underwear? Just because they sell white silk toddler dresses, doesn't mean you have to buy them. Don't build your life around hopelessly stain-prone objects. If you live a white dinner jacket life, your closest and best friend will be the dry cleaner.

Dye-altering chemicals. Many common household products contain chemicals that can alter or destroy the dyes in clothes, carpet, and home furnishings, leaving a bleached or discoloured spot. These include many toilet bowl cleaners, oven cleaners, plant foods, and insecticides (see p. 63). It makes sense to seek safe substitutes for these products, or be extremely careful with them.

Toys. Mean bright colours, loaded with potent dyes. Only you can decide if the benefits offset the risks in such things as coloured modelling clay, crayons, fingerpaints. Many of these products come in washable versions—it pays to check.

Junk. We all have odd bottles, boxes, tins and tubes of aged and often totally unusable stuff lying around—everything from wood stain and spray paint to India ink and liquid shoe dye. I'm convinced we keep some of it just for its stain and torture value! Junk like this always is unleashed—dropped, crushed, broken open—at the worst possible time and place. And the stains from it hurt the worst, because they could have been avoided. Getting rid of this junk is even better than storing it out of reach of children.

Watch Those Liquid Leavings!

Did you ever wonder what happened to the half cup of coffee you didn't finish, the one you left at home, at work, or while travelling? Everyday we buy a drink of some kind, our goal being total consumption, total refreshment. Yet in reality, when we've had enough we just leave the container somewhere with the remains, often where we got tired of it—bus, car, or phone box. Some of us tuck it under, between, or behind something; some of us pour it on the ground, grass, or in the gutter. And some of us just toss it in the bin.

When not dealt with intelligently, this liquid is a real problem. It gets tipped or kicked over, and not only causes stains and stickiness, but draws flies and other insects, and causes falls. Tossed in a waste container, it generally drips through a hole in the plastic bag, rusting or contaminating the waste container, and seeps out into the carpet. Once in the dustbin, it mixes with other liquids and develops into rancid brew fit for chemical warfare! When the dustbin is emptied and the contents compacted, the liquid drips out of the bottom of the dustcart all along the street.

We think our little bit of leftover liquid in the school, or office is all there is. Think of 300 or 3000 other people leaving their half cups of coffee, soft drinks, or water somewhere. That's a lot of buckets of loose liquid someone has to deal with. Who? A mother? The maid? The janitor? The dustman? Once a container of liquid is in your possession, you own it, and if you're decent, you'll take care of it either by drinking it or disposing of it properly. Leaving liquid to be spilled on people or things is pretty low class. If you can't finish it, take it to a sink, or drain and dump it. You'll save someone the nasty job of collecting it, and yourself and others a lot of stains.

Food Control

Twenty years ago, when my company was cleaning homes or commercial buildings, 'spotting' (the official term for cleaning up spills and stains) was a minor assignment. But the amount of carpet we have today and the infiltration of fast food everywhere has swelled spotting into one of the primary pastimes of a cleaner. The majority of stains are from spilled food. It only makes sense to try and **prevent** all we can.

Giving up eating is one possibility, but allow me to suggest a couple of other intake improvements that could lessen food fallout.

Say where! We professional cleaners see dramatic evidence daily that eating is what generates the most and the messiest cleaning. Whether or not eating is allowed there can make a drastic difference in the looks and life expectancy of a room or area and its furnishings. So declare certain places off limits!

Opt for a stainless style of service. How we serve food has a lot to do with it, and buffet meals are about the worst. Offering food this way is an open invitation for people to walk all over the house with it. Where food is carried around and plates are balanced on knees, there will be dropping and spilling and smearing.

Far better to arrange all the eating in one place, at one time, on the surface designed for it—a table. If you must serve the meal elsewhere, make everyone sit down first and bring the food to them.

The right container! Paper plates, cups and like collapsibles start to disintegrate the minute they're put into use. Even if you're a fast eater, they only last long enough to give you time to fill them and assure a spill. Paper plates will always fold on you during second helpings, because by then the cardboard is wet. There goes the carpet, your clothes, or the sofa.

A Couple of Party Pointers

The average party generates 31 stains, 12 of which are on the best furniture and at least half of which have a red dye base; plus 4 broken and 17 items lost or left behind, 3 scratches, countless pounds of scattered litter and waste, and three long-distance calls on your bill.

The most obvious but least practised party precaution is to triple the waste containers throughout the party area, outside and in. Every guest (even the drunks) will look for a disposal site first, and if there's one at his elbow, he will make use of it, and others will follow suit. Likewise, once one slob slings a sausage on to your best cloth, others will follow—you can count on it.

The second secret (secret because even though everyone knows it, no one does it) is that there is more to life and human affairs than trying to decide what and how much to eat. Limit the hors d'oeuvres and drinks to a non-messy, select group. Two kinds of

sandwiches and a couple of drink choices are plenty. More, means indecision and waste in a guest's hand, and a mess later on yours.

At your next party put plenty of waste bins around and pile up fewer goodies, and you'll have much less of a house hangover!

Car Stains

Does your car give 15 stains to the gallon? The more comfortable cars become, the more we live in them. Driving tests should really make us prove ourselves in all the real-life situations we encounter: driving while drinking coffee or cola, while eating, feeding the baby, putting on make-up, writing, adjusting the radio, reading maps, quieting the children, trying to wipe the windscreen. My brother reconditions car interiors professionally and claims he can tell age, sex, religion, marital status, employment, hobbies, etc, from the mess and stains left behind in a vehicle. The odds in favour of spills triple in a car. *Everything* spills—if not straight away, just brake sharply, turn right, do a hill start or change lanes and it will. Almost any activity performed while driving is guaranteed to produce spots and stains.

The good news is that cars have only a couple of surfaces to stain. The bad news is, who carries any stain-removal equipment with them? So spots set. The answer: I keep a small can of aerosol solvent spotter such as K2r for grease stains, and a plastic spray bottle of all-purpose cleaner and several clean towels in my boot, along with a pair of gloves and overalls.

I keep a good supply of wet wipes in the glove box, because clean hands do a lot to prevent spots and stains, and one of those miniature carpet sweepers for crumbs. Crumbs from biscuits or crisps, for example, have grease in them, which will ooze out when the sun heats things up.

Then at first chance to stop after they happen, I get those spills and spots before they have a chance to become stains.

Camouflage

If you've ever owned a white sofa and a black cat, you'll know why this is a good idea. Some colours and patterns don't just show every little mark and stain, they advertise it wholesale. Others can hide a host of ills and maybe even the whole cat. Here's how to select clothes, flooring, wallpaper or furniture:

Colour. Earth colours in medium tones—not too light or too dark—are the best soil and stain hiders. White, yellow, and pastels show dark soil and stains the worst.

Leading a Spotless Existence

We all do stupid things that get us into stain trouble. Here are a few of the bad habits it's well worth your while to break:

★ Ignoring any spill (even water)

★ Letting the baby run around 'just for a few minutes' with no nappy

★ Tossing half-empty liquid anything into a wastepaper basket

★ Leaving a wet paint lid anywhere

★ Saving those miniature sachets of salad cream or jam from the last holiday flight

★ Carrying an uncapped pen or marker around the house

★ Touching anything but a napkin after you've eaten with your fingers

★ Swaddling the duty-free Campari you're hoping to sneak through customs in your best dressing gown

★ Believing the baggage handlers can't possibly break the extra-strong garlic dressing bundled securely inside your Samsonite case

★ Using your beloved picnic rug to cushion the gallon of home-made red wine in the boot

★ Eating take-away spare ribs in slow-moving traffic

★ Eating anything while wearing white

★ Trying to sneak a sip of coffee while walking down the hall

★ Thinking you can eat a pizza without six napkins

★ Balancing a drink on the dashboard 'just while I fasten the seat belt'

★ Leaving the borscht boiling while you answer the phone

★ Putting the open bottle of furniture polish on the stairs

★ Ordering spaghetti while wearing a silk tie

★ Leaving the roller tray of paint at the foot of the ladder

★ Moving the ladder without taking the tin of paint down first

★ Slamming the front door with briefcase and mug in hand

★ Leaving anything until later

Pattern. This is the original way to make things hard to see—ask any anaconda. Small, dense patterns hide stains better than large designs. Mottled, multi-hued fabrics like tweed disguise just about everything, while a large expanse of solid colour will show the slightest imperfection.

Texture. A slight texture will improve the smudge-hiding ability of most surfaces, from carpet, to worktop, to walls and ceilings. An irregular surface reflects light in different directions, and makes spots and stains hard to see. Sculptured carpet, for example, is much more concealing than plush-cut pile. An orange-peel textured ceiling hides flyspecks and exploded champagne far better than stark, perfectly smooth paint.

Moral of the story: If you have a young family, it may be in your best interests to seek out a wall covering with flecks of pea green, stained-carrot orange, and handprint brown.

It's nice to know that most prevention doesn't involve any extra effort or expense, just a tiny bit of thought and planning.

PART II

WHAT'S IT ON?

An Important Part of the Answer to
'How Do I Get It Out?'

Some stains come out so easily, we're amazed. Others elude our every effort, and it's hard to tell where we went wrong. The truth is that there are a lot of different materials out there, and each one reacts differently to stains and stain removal techniques. When confronted with a stain, we immediately think: 'What shall I use to get it out?'—but the question we should ask first is: 'What exactly **is** the stain (see pp. 156/158), and **what is in on**?' A lot of ruined treasures tossed in dustbins and on to rubbish tips testify how many of us make rash moves and snap judgments here.

This section will help you handle correctly, identify, and prevent damage to all the common surfaces where stains are found. The majority of stain problems occur on textiles, so a lot of attention is given to these soft, porous materials. But also look at the hard surfaces that pose a stain problems.

Soft Surfaces

You just can't generalise, even on the way to approach specific fabrics. Every textile begins as some kind of fibre—plant, animal, or man-made—but two fabrics made from the same fibre aren't necessarily treated the same. There are a great many types of silk, for example. Some are sturdy and easy to care for, others extremely delicate and almost impossible to clean. The way a fibre is spun, woven, dyed and finished makes a big difference to how durable, colourfast, and cleanable it is. Any lining, interfacing, or trimming complicates the issue further. Knowing that a suit is made of wool, for instance, doesn't tell the whole story, because a little bit of vinyl or suede piping or a chalk stripe of acetate thread can drastically affect the correct way to treat it. To make things worse, the modern science that can make paper look like steel, gravel like granite, and plastic like pine, has no problem making synthetics that imitate silk perfectly, and would-be wools that could fool a mother sheep. Which means most of us amateurs are instantly confused (we're told not to use ammonia on silk, but is it really silk, or is it rayon, nylon, or acetate, we wonder?). Ninety per cent of us can't tell by the look or feel, so may I direct you towards one of your best friends in stain removal—the label. A fabric care label is the safest way to tell how to treat a garment.

Love Those Labels

Care labels on clothes and household textiles carry valuable information about how to treat each item. The Laundry Code was revised in 1986 and items bought before then will carry old-style labels. The chart below shows old and new symbols.

TEXTILE CARE LABELLING CODE

Old   New
symbol symbol

White cotton and linen articles without special finishes.

Cotton, linen or viscose articles without special finishes where colours are fast at 60°C.

Nylon; polyester/cotton mixtures; polyester cotton and viscose articles with special finishes; cotton/acrylic mixtures.

Cotton, linen or viscose articles, where colours are fast at 40°C but not at 60°C. Absence of bar denotes maximum machine action.

Acrylics, acetate and triacetate, including mixtures with wool; polyester/wool blends. Single bar denotes medium machine action.

Wool, wool mixed with other fibres; silk. Two bars denote minimum machine action.

Hand wash (do not machine wash).

Do not wash.

DRY CLEANING SYMBOLS

(A) Normal goods dry cleanable in all solvents.

(P) Normal goods dry cleanable in perchloroethylene, Solvent R113, white spirit, and Solvent R11. If letter is underlined, do not coin op.

(F) Normal goods dry cleanable in Solvent R113 and white spirit. If letter is underlined, do not coin op.

Do not dry clean.

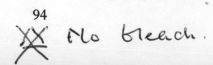

No bleach.

For carpeting, you may just have to keep track of what you bought, because there isn't usually anything anywhere on it to tell you what it is and how to care for it. The newest generation of nylons (the 'stain-resist' carpets), especially, have some very specific cleaning instructions that have to be carefully followed or you'll void the warranty. So keep any cleaning information they give you when you buy carpet or furniture safely on file, so you'll know what to do when that inevitable emergency happens (or for that matter, what to do by way of regular cleaning).

What If There Isn't a Label?

Most of us have learned to recognise cotton and poly/cotton blends, and wool. (If your jacket smells like a wet dog when you come in out of the rain, it's probably wool.) But what do you do when there's no label and you haven't a clue? Use old-fashioned guesswork, and proceed cautiously in the direction it leads you. Since 90 per cent of carpet is now nylon, assume that yours is until you find out differently. Most moderately priced upholstered furniture and virtually all car upholstery can be wet-cleaned, so try shampooing in an out-of-the-way place to see if it'll be all right.

Trying to work out the fibre content of an unlabelled piece can be a tricky business, however. There are imitation silks around that even a silkworm wouldn't suspect. But blends are the real bugbear. Without extensive testing, it's very difficult to tell which fibres are blended in a particular fabric. Professional cleaners are trained to do it, and if you have a carpet, curtain or piece of clothing you're not sure about, the safest approach is to turn it over to a pro. Certain fabrics, such as brocade, velvet, silk chiffon, taffeta, and watered silk are just plain hard (or impossible) to clean successfully without special training and equipment. If it's valuable, and especially if it's an antique, give the job to an expert dry cleaner—the peace of mind will be worth the price, and the piece will still be worth keeping afterwards.

For spots and spills on everyday unlabelled fabric, here are some rules that can help keep you out of trouble.

1. Pre-test. I've said it before, but I don't want you to forget it! Use an inconspicuous part of the garment, carpet, or furniture to pre-test the prospective spot remover (even water). Put on a drop of solution that's twice as strong as you intend to use, let it sit for longer than you would in the actual stain removal process, then blot it out. If there's any colour change or fabric damage, STOP there—don't use it.

2. If it's delicate, go easy. Loose or extremely fine weaves, antique cloth, brocades, etc. can be damaged by rough handling. Tamp, scrape, or dry-brush very gently (if at all) to avoid fraying, bruising, or dislocating fibres. Avoid the use of heat or harsh chemicals if gentler methods will do the job.

3. If it's shiny, be extra wary of using water. Some lustrous fabrics such as taffeta or fine silk water spot like mad, and should only be treated with dry spotters. Some moirés (fabrics with a wavy, watery look) are **ruined** by water. The safest approach for such tender morsels is to take them in for expert dry cleaning.

4. Get professional help if you need it—these people are your friends. A professional cleaner can not only identify your carpet fibre, a good one can even tell you which generation of nylon it is! A dry cleaner you use regularly should be willing to help you distinguish between items you should bring in and those where you can handle simple spots yourself. Even if you have to pay for the advice once, it's worth knowing which way to turn.

For a full explanation of the stain-removal techniques specified in this section, see Chapter 4.
(For descriptions of the solvents, see Chapter 5.)

A I said earlier, fibre is the starting point for all fabrics. There are two basic types: **natural**, which come from plants or animals; and **man-made**, which come from a laboratory.

Natural Fibres

Natural fibres from plants are called cellulose fibres, and this group includes cotton and linen. Animal fibres are known as protein fibres and include silk and wool. Cellulose fibres tend to be absorbent, so they pick up stains easily, but they usually give them up without a serious fight. Protein fibres are fairly stain-resistant, but also fairly sensitive to chemicals, so you can't always use the most effective weapons in your stainbuster's arsenal on them.

Here are some general guidelines on different types of fabrics and how you can expect them to react.

Fibre; Found in	Stain characteristics	Cautions
Cotton Light- and medium-weight garments, linens, handkerchiefs, loose covers, curtains; often blended with polyester in permanent-press garments	Very absorbent, so it picks up stains easily, but also responds well to removal measures; subject to mildew	Handles most solvents well but is sensitive to acids (don't use vinegar on it), withstands heat well
Linen Blouses, dresses, summer suits, household linens, and other articles	Absorbent, so it stains easily, but not as bad as cotton	Shares cotton's sensitivity to acids and mildew; high heat is fine
Ramie Light- and medium-weight garments. Blended with cotton in sweaters	More stain-resistant than cotton or linen	Sensitive to acids, but fairly mildew-resistant; handles heat well
Silk Light- and medium-weight garments, scarves, home furnishings	Fairly stain-resistant due to the smoothness of the fibre. Susceptible to yellowing from alkalis, chlorine bleach, high ironing temperatures, perspiration, and exposure to sunlight; stain removal often difficult because silk is sensitive to so many different chemicals	Many silks water-spot, and require dry cleaning. Damaged by ammonia, vinegar, harsh alkaline cleaners and chlorine bleach
Wool (including alpaca, angora, camel hair, mohair, and vicuna). Light-, medium- and heavy-weight garments, coats, blankets, carpet	Naturally water-repellent so it tends to resist many stains; but removal of stains from wool is difficult because of its sensitivity to chemicals	Damaged by ammonia, alcohol, harsh alkaline cleaners, chlorine bleach—most woollens require dry cleaning or delicate handwashing, cool air drying

Man-made Fibres

Though some man-made fibres were produced on an experimental basis as early as the mid-1800s, they've come into widespread use only in the past 40 years. In that short time the list of man-made fibres has expanded to include 21 generic names and more than 200 trade names, so it gets a bit confusing. Because of their non-absorbent nature, most man-made fibres are fairly resistant to water-based staining agents, but some of them actually attract oily and greasy stains. Synthetics also tend to hold on to stains tighter than natural fibres—they don't give them up without a fight. While synthetics are generally resistant to chemical damage, a few are critically sensitive to certain chemicals, and most don't tolerate stain removal procedures involving heat well.

Fibre; Found in	Stain characteristics	Cautions
Acetate (Dicel, Lansil, Fibroceta etc) Lingerie, linings, curtains, upholstery, fibre fill for duvets, pillows, and mattress pads	Good resistance to stains and mildew; susceptible to colour fading and dye running	Damaged by acetone, vinegar, alcohol; sensitive to heat; most acetates must be dry-cleaned or washed as delicates
Acrylic (Acrilan, Orlon, Courtelle, Dralon etc) All kinds of clothing (especially sweaters), pile fabrics, blankets, carpet, curtains	Good resistance to stains and mildew	Sensitive to heat—always use warm water, dryer, and iron settings
Modacrylic (Crylor, Dynel etc) Deep pile coats, blankets, children's sleepwear, fake fur (stuffed toys)	Good resistance to stains and mildew	Extremely heat-sensitive—no hot-air drying, always use lowest iron setting
Nylon (BriNylon, Cantrese, Enkalon etc) Blouses, dresses, hosiery, lingerie, jackets, bedspreads, curtains, sleeping bags, tents, carpet	Very good resistance to most stains, especially oily and greasy ones; white nylon will yellow in sunlight, and will pick up fugitive dyes if laundered with coloured garments	Somewhat heat-sensitive—hot water okay but use warm dryer, iron settings

Fibre; Found in	Stain characteristics	Cautions
Polyester (Terylene, Dacron, Crimplene, Tactel, Trevira etc) Blended extensively with cotton, rayon, and wool for use in all types of garments, especially permanent-press items; also fibre fill for pillows, jackets, etc.	Good resistance to non-oily stains, but attracts oily stains; resistant to sunlight, mildew, and perspiration	Moderately heat-sensitive—warm water, dryer, and iron settings are best choice
Rayon (Viscose, Vincel, Evlan, Darelle, Fibro etc) Blouses, dresses, lingerie, rainwear, trousers, sportswear	Good stain resistance; susceptible to mildew	Slightly susceptible to acids (use vinegar sparingly); resin-treated rayon may be damaged by chlorine bleach; use medium heat
Spandex (Lycra, Spanzelle) Foundation garments, swimwear, sportswear, ski pants, support hose, elasticised fabrics	Good resistance to stains, body oils, perspiration	Damaged (de-elasticised!) by chlorine bleach; very heat-sensitive—use lowest dryer and iron settings
Triacetate (Arnel, Tricel) Permanent-pleat garments, dresses, flannel, jersey, taffeta, textured knits, tricot, sportswear	Good stain resistance, but subject to mildew	Damaged by vinegar, acetone, alcohol; withstands high heat well

Three Troublesome Fabrics Worth a Closer Look

Silk. Silk fabrics vary enormously in the care they require and how they respond to cleaning. Though most have to be dry cleaned, some silks can be washed successfully, while others bleed dye at the drop of a hat. As noted earlier silk fibre is sensitive to acids, alkaline detergents, ammonia and chlorine bleach (this list includes almost all of the really potent stain removers). Silk is also extra-delicate, easily abraded and very likely to water spot. If you get a serious stain on a silk garment, take it to a professional cleaner. If it's one you usually wash, you can try the stain-removal methods recommended for that particular stain, but take it slowly and carefully.

Wool. Doesn't like rough handling or harsh chemicals either, and that includes heat, alkaline detergents, ammonia, alcohol, and chlorine bleach. It's more tolerant of water. Although a 100 per cent wool garment will probably shrink when soaked with water, wool blended with synthetic fibres can often be washed on a delicate cycle, or hand washed although shrinkage is still possible. Many woollens and worsteds will also stand up to a little tamping. You need to be very careful about rubbing or scrubbing wool when wet, though, as it can 'felt' and shrink. You should be able to remove many stains from wool yourself, but if it's a valuable piece, call in a professional cleaner. Coffee has an affinity with wool fibre, and is particularly hard to remove from light-coloured woollens.

Velvet. Soft, plushy surfaces can be deceptive. Many of the new synthetic (acrylic and nylon) velvet and velour upholstery fabrics wear like iron, and clean like stainless steel. And cotton velveteen is usually pretty durable, and can be washed in the same way as any delicate fabric.

But the older velvets, many of them made of silk, wool, and other delicate fibres, are very easily damaged and require special care. Some velvets never recover from being hung on the wrong kind of hanger, so they'll definitely be ruined by careless cleaning. If you have an older garment with a velvet collar, an antique chair, or any velvet you're unsure of, take it to a professional.

With any plush fabric, take care not to crush the pile or create a bald spot with harsh scrubbing. And when you've finished spotting, brush all the pile in the same direction, or it'll dry with a splotchy look.

Other Sensitive Softies

Leather. Finished leather, the kind that's been dyed and has a smooth, lustrous finish, resists stains fairly well. Always go easy with water on leather. On finished leather, try wiping spots off with a plain dry cloth—you'll find that many soils succumb to this simple treatment. Wipe any remaining dirt away with a sponge or cloth dampened with lukewarm water and a mild soap, such as saddle soap. Then buff dry with a clean cloth. When a leather item

Those Temperamental Ties!

The man's tie. I agree—what could be more stupid than a piece of overpriced cloth tied around our neck to prove to the public that we are dressed up. No wonder it gets so many stains—it's in the perfect place to drag through everything and catch drips, dandruff, food fallout, and grease from hands when it's straightened. Cleaning your own ties (especially silk) is treading on treacherous ground. These little devils are cut on the bias, so the fabric distorts very easily, and most have a lining that's prone to wrinkle and shrink. Even professionals have a hard time cleaning a silk tie so it looks right afterwards.

Steer clear of madras, too. The dye runs all too easily. Wool is more workable—you can usually spot these yourself. Just follow the instructions in Part III for that particular stain, including all the cautions for wool. Then press the tie if it needs it, using a damp cloth.

I remove minor grease spots from washable ties using washing-up liquid diluted with water.

When one of my favourite ties gets a major stain, or just starts to look tacky, I give the dry cleaner a go at it. If it's a plain old everyday tie, I simply replace it.

To keep your ties looking as good as possible for as long as possible, it doesn't hurt to cut down on tie-endangering habits and practices, such as letting the end drop on to your plate when you bend over to sit down at the table... taking it off and hanging it on doorknobs or chair backs... tossing it on the back seat, or into an overstuffed drawer, or on to a cluttered dressing table... stuffing it carelessly into a suitcase (too close to the aftershave), or closing the suitcase on it. And don't be ashamed to tuck your tie inside your shirt when you sit down to soup or a juicy hamburger. (You could also switch to cravats or bow ties.)

gets a serious stain such as ink, dye, paint, glue or nail polish, rush it to a professional cleaner. The cleaning process also restores the oils to the skin to keep it from drying out and cracking, and should be done every year or two in any case.

Unfinished leathers such as suede are another matter. These have no protective finish, so they slurp up stains fast and hold on to

them forever. You can't do much about removing spots from this kind of leather yourself, beyond brushing it with a suede brush. Get your unfinished leather treated with a water repellent to minimise stain penetration, and take it in for professional cleaning as soon as it's needed. Don't wait until there's a lot of heavy, ingrained dirt for the cleaner to deal with. But bear in mind that not all dry cleaners are equipped to deal with leathers and furs; look for a cleaner who specialises.

With all leather garments, wearing a scarf to protect the collar from body oils and make-up will help avoid stains and greatly extend the time between cleanings. (Now we know why all those WWI pilots wore scarves.)

Carpet and Upholstery

Of everything we own, we probably treat carpets the worst. We trample on them; push heavy furniture around on them; and drop, slop, spill, and drip everything from gravy, to grape juice, to axle grease on them. It's a testimony to the carpet industry that they stay looking a good as they do, in spite of us.

The big drawback when it comes to de-staining carpet and upholstery is that spotters can't be flushed through the fabric as they can in most garments. It's a real help to be able to flood water or spotting chemicals through the fabric from the back side to the front, so the stain is pushed back out the way it came in. With

102

clothes, too, you can use as much liquid as needed to 'wash' stains out of the fabric. But with carpets and upholstery (and some garments with padding, lining, etc.) there isn't that kind of freedom, so techniques have to be altered.

Because you're forced to work from the face of the fabric, be careful not to drive stains deeper as you go. Be extra sure to use absorbents and blotting action to remove as much of the stain as possible before applying any chemical. And here especially dry-brushing and scraping should be done in such a way as to lift dirt and stain matter up and away from the fibres, rather than force it into the pile.

Be careful also not to over-wet the fabric, because getting the underlay, furniture filling material (or garment lining) saturated can create a lot of headaches. Solvents attack many of the foam fillings and latex adhesives used in carpet and furniture construction, and colours can bleed out of wet backing and filling materials and stain the cover fabric. So use as little solvent as possible, and compensate by leaving it on the fabric longer and using gentle agitation to break down the stain. Since all chemicals have to be blotted out, rinsed, and the rinse water blotted out, too, it makes sense to go easy on liquid. Stains that reappear in carpets and upholstery are largely a result of not enough blotting (see p. 000). When you pour on liquid and don't blot it all out, it carries the stain deep down into the fabric, where it will wick back up as the item dries. The spot may look fine when it's wet, but a quickfire stain-removal job on carpet or upholstery will usually reappear.

In general, you can use the procedures outlined for 'Dry cleanables' in 'How to go about it' on carpet, upholstered furniture, and vehicle upholstery. Just remember to rinse and blot thoroughly, as outlined above, and you'll be down there taking out carpet spots like a pro.

Carpet spots that reappear. We've all had freshly cleaned spots in carpet that miraculously (and maddeningly) reappear a few hours, or even days, after cleaning. What this means is that they weren't completely removed in the first place. The surface of the pile was clean, but stain matter or detergent residue was buried deep in the carpet. As the pile dries, the water evaporates from the tips of the yarn first, which prompts more moisture to travel up from deep in the carpet. If any stain material remains, it migrates up to the yarn tips along with the moisture, and leaves the face of the carpet stained again when it's dry.

When it comes to oil and grease stains, if you don't get it all out, the oil itself resurfaces as you walk on the carpet, and becomes highly visible as it attracts and holds dirt.

To avoid reappearing carpet spots, clean and rinse anything beyond surface spots thoroughly, using enough liquid to get down to the roots of the pile without soaking through into the underlay. When you've finished, put a thick, clean, absorbent towel on the freshly cleaned spot and weigh it down with a heavy book or a brick. Leave it there until the carpet is thoroughly dry, and all the moisture and any remaining stain stuff will travel up into the towel.

Oriental Rugs (and Other Valuable Floor Coverings)

If you have a valuable oriental or a prized antique rug, don't be too quick to start spotting it yourself. There are so many possible combinations of dyes and fibres, some of them pretty sensitive to rough handling, that you can't generalise about the care of art underfoot. Use a professional cleaner who specialises in cleaning such pieces, and count it money well spent.

Mattresses, Pillows and Other Padded Surfaces

The cover fabric on most mattresses stains from just about any kind of spill, and deep cleaning is difficult, so protection is the key. All mattresses should be covered with a mattress pad (and you might well want to put a waterproof mattress cover under that for young children or the bed-bound). Then you can soak, wash, apply enzyme detergent etc, at will to any stains on the pad and the surface of the mattress itself will be protected. If the mattress cover is stained, it can be lightly shampooed, but don't get the padding underneath wet. To remove stains from mattresses, treat them like upholstered furniture. Use the 'Drycleanables' instructions in 'How to go about it,' be careful not to over-wet, and blot thoroughly to remove any chemicals you use. Feather the edges to avoid leaving a water spot.

For pillows and duvets, protection with covers will do a lot to prevent staining. Isolated spots can be lightly sponged with the appropriate chemical, then rinsed, blotted, and feathered, as described for mattresses. The same is true of quilted items, stuffed toys, etc.

Although many pillow manufacturers recommend dry cleaning, most pillows can be successfully machine washed and dried if your machine is big enough (use the delicate or gentle cycle, low heat). Check the care label if there is one for instructions. Be forewarned that pillows may go lumpy when washed. Duvets should be dry cleaned or professionally laundered.

Skin. Well, it is a soft surface isn't it? And it does get stained. The best way to take care of stains on your hands is to avoid them. Wear rubber gloves for such stain-prone activities as polishing shoes or picking blackberries. Or if gloves cramp your style, rub one of the 'liquid glove' products into your hands to seal out the mess before you change the oil in your car or paint the back door. When you've finished the messy task, all the grease or paint or whatever will wash off. For removing stains that do get to your skin, the waterless hand cleaner mechanics use work quite well. Just remember that skin is sensitive and it absorbs chemicals, so don't use strong stain-removing solutions and solvents on your hands or any skin. Better to wash with a mild soap, put on some hand lotion, and wait for the stuff to loosen by itself than to risk an allergic reaction or absorption of some dangerous chemical.

Paper. True, paper isn't really soft—but most papers aren't really hard either. For the most part paper is extremely porous, though, so it sucks up stains like a sponge. We've learned to deal with most paper stains with pencil rubbers, correction fluid, or retyping. And many non-greasy spots can be gently wiped away with a clean, damp cloth, if it's a paper with rag content, such as watermarked bond. Even if you spill coffee on your essay, the day it's due, there's hope. Sponge the paper quickly with a mild vinegar solution, then press it with a warm iron. Use blotting paper or a cloth when doing this, to prevent scorching. It may not look quite pristine, but it'll be better than it was.

For inexpensive posters or prints (or any paper) marked with fingerprints or oil stains, first rub the spot with an art gum eraser, then sponge with lighter fluid or spray with K2r. Don't try these tactics on valuable prints, first editions or watercolours—take them to a professional art restorer. And make sure all art prints or objects are professionally glassed and framed or cased for protection.

Wallpaper. Most 'wallpaper' isn't paper any more. Most of it is either solid vinyl or vinyl-coated paper or cloth. Even vinyl wall coverings vary in their cleanability, with the higher-priced ones usually being the most stain resistant and cleanable. Solid vinyl wallcoverings can withstand quite a bit of rubbing and scrubbing, while the cheaper, thin-coated papers can be damaged by any heavy-handed stain removal procedures.

The first step in removing stains from wall coverings is to try dry wiping, either with an art gum eraser from artists' shops, or a pencil eraser. Next, try wiping gently with neutral detergent solution, but be careful not to wet the seams. For sturdier papers, more aggressive stain removal techniques can follow, using the chemicals recommended in Part III. Be sure to pre-test all spotters in an out-of-the-way place first, though—some stain solvents make the dyes in wall coverings run, and the pattern can be scrubbed completely off some cheaper papers. See 'Vinyl fabrics' for chemicals that shouldn't be used on this popular plastic.

If you still have wallpaper up from the days when it **was** just porous paper with patterns dyed on, you probably won't be able to use any water on it. Wipe it down with a dry sponge.

Vinyl fabrics. Including furniture and vehicle upholstery, clothing, etc. The safest course is to wipe it with neutral detergent solution. Since vinyl is fairly non-absorbent, most stains will come out with a little patience. Never use dry cleaning fluid, lacquer thinner, acetone, or nail polish remover on vinyl. Any kind of volatile solvent can soften the plastic or leach out the plasticisers, leaving the surface dry and brittle. And steel wool or any kind of abrasive or harsh scraping can remove the pattern from the surface, or score it. Applying petroleum jelly (leave on for up to 30 minutes) often helps lift stains off vinyl.

Hard Surfaces

Stains aren't as big a threat to most hard surfaces as they are to textiles. Many of the hard surfaces we deal with, such as window glass, chrome, porcelain, and glazed ceramic tiles, are so non-absorbent as to be almost stainproof. Slightly more porous surfaces such as painted walls, vinyl floors, and plastic laminate ('Formica') worktops are susceptible to some types of stains, but are by and large impervious to spills. Removal from these relatively non-permeable surfaces often involves no more than a quick swipe with a damp cloth. If you have highly porous hard surfaces such as raw wood, concrete, brick, or stone that aren't properly sealed against stain penetration, read Chapter 10 before you do anything else.

For stains on hard surfaces, use the same solvents and cleaning chemicals you do on textiles; and adapt your attack to the surface you're working on. For instance, hairspray will take ballpoint ink off marble just as well as it will off a white shirt. But instead of flushing it through a fabric, you'll have to spray it on, let it sit a few seconds, scrub gently with a white nylon abrasive pad to work it loose, then wipe it away.

The pre-test rule applies to hard surfaces, too. Try any questionable cleaners in a hidden area first to make sure they won't do any harm. Don't use strong solvents like acetone and lacquer thinner on paint, vinyl, varnished wood, or plastic (including plastic laminates such as Formica). Solvents can soften and damage these materials. You can safely use such volatile solvents to remove stubborn stains like paint, nail polish and glue from glass, chrome, china, porcelain, quarry tile floors, and other chemically resistant surfaces. Here are some tips on how to deal with specific surfaces.

Raw wood. The only good advice I can give you regarding raw wood is: don't have any! Some designers like to leave certain types

107

of wood planking raw and unfinished. While this can result in a nice natural look and aroma, it won't stay handsome for long. Any kind of stain will sink into the porous surface, and be very difficult to remove. A dye stain, such as ink or food dye, will be virtually impossible. The pores in wood are designed to transport liquid, and transport it they will—many stains will sink in so deep you can't even sand them away. And you can't use a lot of water on raw wood without swelling the grain.

Soft woods stain worst of all, but all wood should be protected with a sealer or finish of some kind, the best probably being polyurethane. Polyurethane or varnish with a stain finish will keep your wood looking expensive while preventing stain penetration.

For stains on existing raw wood, try the spotting chemicals recommended for that specific stain in Part III, followed by light sanding if necessary. Then get a coat of sealer on.

NOTE: Much so-called 'wood' panelling isn't really wood at all, except for the cheap plywood or chipboard base sheet underneath. The rich-looking grained surface is actually a thin sheet of vinyl or paper bonded to the panel, with a 'picture' of real wood printed on it. The dead giveaway is that the same grain patterns repeat from one sheet to the next. If your 'wood' panelling is of this type, follow the instructions for vinyl under 'Vinyl fabrics' and 'Wallpaper' (p. 106).

Raw stone, brick, and concrete. Ditto what I said for wood. The only masonry surface I wouldn't seal would be something extremely hard and smooth like polished granite. Bourneseal can be used on some stonework, but test before use. For concrete, brick and rough stonework, use the concrete cleaners and stain removers sold by DIY stores as brick or patio cleaner. These are dilute hydrochloric acid, so be careful.

Once you get it clean, put a coat or two of masonry seal such as Cuprinol Water Seal on to keep future stains from sinking in.

To remove fresh oil stains from concrete, sprinkle them with cat litter, grind it in with your foot, and let it sit until the oil is absorbed. A final wipe with turps should take care of any remaining traces.

Vinyl floors. The newer vinyl floors are more stain-resistant than their predecessors. The top layer of clear vinyl on these floors is so thick, hard, and glossy that most stains won't penetrate it. Here, too, avoid strong solvents like acetone and lacquer thinner, which will soften the plastic, but most household stains and chemicals will wipe off with no damage. If you have an older floor, it's probably sheet vinyl, vinyl composition tiles or maybe even vinyl asbestos tiles. If it's really old, it may be linoleum. These materials aren't as impervious to stains and chemical damage, so they need protection. If you keep a good coat of floor finish (such as Johnson's Klear) on these floors, stains are very likely be confined to the wax. If you get a bad stain, all you have to do is remove the old polish with floor stripper bought from a commercial cleaning company or janitorial supplies wholesaler. Then rewax—the flooring material underneath will be untouched.

Don't use steel wool, powdered cleansers, or anything abrasive on any type of vinyl flooring, except as a last resort. And watch what you're doing when you scrape. If you do get a stain on linoleum, try linseed oil or gentle scrubbing with a Scotchbrite pad. And if all else fails, put in a new patch of flooring.

One very troublesome stain on vinyl flooring is caused by colour bleeding from a vinyl-backed mat or rug that is kept in one place for too long. The vinyl contains plasticisers to keep it soft, and they will eventually migrate out of dark-coloured mat backing into the vinyl of a light-coloured floor, leaving an ugly stain. Such stains can often be lightened by scrubbing, bleaching and exposure to sunlight but are often impossible to remove entirely. The only real cure is prevention—don't leave mats or rugs with dark-coloured backings in one place too long, especially in front of a glass patio door or anywhere else where the sun warms the floor.

Plastic laminates (Formica, etc). The plastic laminates used on worktops are quite hard and non-porous, but will still absorb some stains. One cure for worktop stains is to have patience. A stain like grape juice will look pretty dreadful on the first day, but will lighten with each successive damp wiping, and will often disappear completely after a few days of regular cleaning. This approach is far preferable to attacking the stain with harsh chemicals, which take their toll on the surface of the plastic.

For a stubborn stain, try a poultice of bleaching powdered cleanser such as Ajax. Mix the cleanser into a paste with water, smear it on the stain, and let it dry. When dry, wipe it carefully to avoid scratching the plastic, and you'll usually find that the poultice has absorbed the stain. If any remains, repeat the application. (Baking soda and lemon juice will work, too.)

Stubborn stains on plastic laminate can be bleached with a 1:5 mixture of household bleach and water, but don't let it sit for more than a few minutes. You can also use scouring powder to remove bad stains, but don't get into the habit of scrubbing laminate with abrasive cleansers, coloured nylon pads, or steel wool; they'll scratch the surface and make it rough and porous. If you have to use scouring powder to remove a bad stain, be as gentle as possible. If the surface gets scratched from the cleanser, you'll have to restore the finish by polishing it with polishing compound like T-Cut, from car accessory shops. Coating scratched laminate with car polish also helps make it smoother and more stain-resistant. For severe damage like burns or bubbles from cigarettes or hot pans, get a professional kitchen installer to 'plug' the hole with new piece.

Glassfibre. We run across glassfibre in everything from motor-boats to curtain fabrics, these days, but our biggest concern when it comes to stain removal, is usually moulded glassfibre bath panels, shower enclosures, vanity tops, and the like. The mistake most often made with things like this is scrubbing them with harsh chemicals or abrasive cleansers and coloured nylon pads, which make them rough and porous. Then every little speck of hard water, soap scum, or rust sinks in or sticks like glue. If you have glassfibre fixtures that have been abused in this way, try restoring the finish by polishing with T-Cut from car accessory shops, then coat the surface with a good car wax. This will make the surface smooth and glossy again.

The right approach to take here is to use a J-cloth and all-purpose cleaner for stubborn spots and stains. If you use acid bath and tile cleaners to remove hard-water stains, be sure to rinse the acid away afterwards, then wax the surface well to slow down future buildup. Don't use harsh acids like lavatory cleaner on glassfibre, and avoid the use of strong solvents such as acetone or lacquer thinner.

Fake marble. These vanity tops and sinks are very popular with home builders, but you have to be careful not to damage them in your attempts to clean them. All the instructions given above for glassfibre apply.

Paint and varnish. By this I mean anything—including walls, panelling, painted furniture, and kitchen cabinets—that has a finish such as paint, varnish, lacquer, shellac, or urethane. As you might suspect, there's a great difference in the stain-resistance and cleanability of finishes like these. If your walls are covered with rough, porous bargain emulsion, don't expect the crayon marks to

come off very well. The thing to remember with paint and varnish is not to use strong solvents, which can soften or damage the finish. Things like lighter fuel, lacquer thinner, and acetone should not be used on painted surfaces. And never use alcohol on shellac. Turps is fine for removing grease and tar from varnish-type finishes and from enamel paint, but it shouldn't be used on matt or silk emulsion or left for long on any paint. Use water-based cleaners on matt or silk finishes; and even then avoid soaking or overaggressive scrubbing—you may end up removing the paint as well as the stain.

Avoid scrubbing, scraping, steel woolling, etc too vigorously on **any** paint or varnish; it could create a dull spot or let the previous colour show through.

Porcelain. This is a slick, hard, glasslike finish, so anything that gets on it usually stays on the surface. It stands up well to most solvents and chemicals, too, so stain removal is generally easy. One caution: don't scrub porcelain baths, sinks, and appliances with harsh scouring powders—some of them can scratch and dull even this tough material.

Do be careful of the things that are near it, though. Because they themselves are so rugged, we sometimes get carried away when working on porcelain sinks or baths, and wreak havoc on the metal fittings and surrounding surfaces. Don't use harsh acids like

111

lavatory cleaner to remove hard water stains in porcelain fixtures—they'll damage the chrome drain fittings. Use Ataka or similar products, sold as kettle cleaners, to remove limescale. Use brick cleaner, with great care, if deposit is very bad. Abrasive nylon pads will also scratch chrome. See precautions under 'Metals' below for stain-removal chemicals and tools that shouldn't be used on chrome and other bathroom metalwork.

Metals. We tend to think of metals as tough and impenetrable, but they do get stained, and many of them can be damaged by common cleaning and stain-removal chemicals. Softer metals like brass, copper, and silver, tarnish readily, and can be worn prematurely by polishing with abrasive metal-polishing creams. Silvo and Brasso, sold under the Duraglit brand name, or Goddard's Long Term Silver Polish, will be easier on them. Silver, brass or copper that's for display only (not used for food service) should be

lacquered to prevent tarnishing. Aluminium, such as anodised window frames, can be lightly oiled with WD-40 to prevent staining and oxidation.

Chrome is so bright and hard, it's tempting to think nothing can hurt it. The truth is, that thin coat of chrome plating on your bathroom taps is more vulnerable than you imagine. If you have sink drains that used to be bright and shiny chrome but are now a dull brass colour or tarnished green, you know what I mean. Scrubbing with abrasive cleaner or nylon pads can scratch and dull chrome fixtures. Over-enthusiastic rubbing with abrasive metal polishes can wear the shiny surface away. Harsh acid bowl cleaners or chlorine bleach will eat little pinholes in chrome fixtures, which show up as dark black or green specks.

Earth tiles. This includes everything from quarry tile floors to the ceramic tiles used for worktops and shower enclosures. Most ceramic tiles, especially those with a shiny glaze, are impervious to just about any stain. The problem, of course, is the grout in between. Choose an epoxy-based grout if you are tiling from scratch. Old, badly stained grout can be removed and replaced with epoxy-based grout. Alternatively scrub stained grout with a good all-purpose cleaner solution and a stiff brush, or use a proprietary grout cleaner from diy stores. Bleaching with a 1:5 dilution of chlorine bleach in water may help, especially for mildew stains in showers (see 'Mildew'). Don't use strong acid masonry cleaners— they eat away the grout cement, and will eventually destroy it.

PART III

HOW TO GO ABOUT IT

The Most Common Spots and Stains and
How to Remove Them

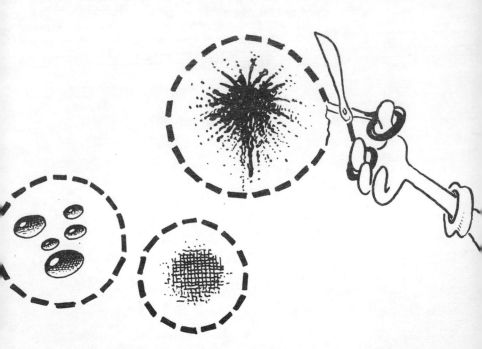

To Adapt the Instructions in This Section to Other Surfaces

To make this book as helpful as possible, the stain removal instructions in the following section are written to apply to the surfaces most commonly stained. Since problem stains occur mostly on clothing, carpet, and upholstered furniture, most of the procedures focus on stain removal from textiles. But if a particular stain (such as pet accidents) is more of a concern on carpet than it is on clothing, the instructions concentrate on carpet. Stain removal from hard surfaces is described only when it's a special problem, or when that's where the stain is mainly found, such as with hard-water stains.

To adapt the instructions in 'How to Go About It' to other types of surfaces as well, see Part II. All the substances used still apply, but you have to adjust the instructions slightly here and there to fit the situation.

For a full explanation of the stain-removal techniques specified in this section, see Chapter 4.
(For descriptions of solvents, see Chapter 5.)

Don't let the fancy chemical terms and detailed directions in the following pages intimidate you—getting rid of most stains is a fairly simple affair. Some of the directions may look involved, but you don't need to do all the steps to take out most stains. Just go from one step to another until the stain is gone, and that's it. A lot of stains will come out with the first step listed, and only the really stubborn ones will call for the whole process. Otherwise, there are just a couple of things to remember:

1. Have a really good look to make sure you've got **all** the stain out before you stop working on it—if there's any left, drying or ironing will probably set it.

2. Don't stop in the middle of a step and leave spotting chemicals in the fabric. If you must stop, go as far as the rinse or flush part of that portion of the instructions, to be sure you get out the last spot remover you used with the recommended rinsing agent before you go off to make a phone call or change a nappy.

3. Unless you're putting the item in the wash immediately, always feather the edges of the spotted area as a last step as soon as the stain is gone, whether you've reached the part of the procedure that calls for feathering or not.

To group fabrics in this section I've used the terms 'washable' and 'dry cleanable.' A **washable** fabric is one you would normally launder and that can stand up to either hand or machine washing. The term **dry cleanable** means those fabrics that will tolerate dry cleaning *only*. Within this group you have to use some judgment as to how much water you use in spot removal. Some dry cleanable fabrics (such as wool) tolerate water fairly well, while others (such as silk or taffeta) can be damaged by water or wet spotters. On any dry clean only fabric, the use of water should be limited to sponging the spot or stain for a few minutes and then air drying— never immerse the whole garment, or soak it in water. You should also limit the time any water-based pastes or poultices stay on there to 30 minutes or less.

WARNING: Before you start to use any chemical solvent, read the safety instructions on pp. 64-66.

117

A Quick Summary of Basic Techniques

Blot. Apply clean white cotton cloths to absorb.

Dry-brush. Brush dry stain matter up and away from the surface lightly with a medium-stiff brush. Vacuum up the rest.

Scrape. Slide a scraper back and forth gently over the surface to break up and remove hardened stains, or to help work solvents in.

Freeze. Apply ice to the spot to freeze it hard or place in freezer; then fracture it, reduce it to crumbs, and scrape it away with a butter knife.

Soak. Immerse in water or the specified solution for at least 30 minutes. Soak dry cleanables, carpets, etc, by applying a cloth dampened with the solution.

Poultice. Mix the materials into a paste, apply it to the stain, let it dry, then wipe it away.

Sponge. Lay the stained article face down on a pad of clean white absorbent cloth and use another such pad, dampened with the spotter, to push the spotter through the stained fabric into the pad below.

Tamp. Spread the stained fabric face up on a smooth level surface and strike the stain with the flat face of a spotting brush.

Flush. Apply the specified liquid liberally to the back side of the stain with a spray or squeeze bottle, to flush it through the fabric.

Rinse. Rinse well with water or the specified solution to remove all stain and spotter residue.

Sponge-rinse. Sponge water through the spot with a clean cloth pad or, in the case of carpet and upholstery, sponge on clear water and then blot it out.

Feather. To rinse and dry a spot from the outside in, to blend in the edges and avoid leaving a ring.

Acids

What is it? Aggressive acids as found in toilet bowl cleaners, and car batteries (and vomit and urine, as well).

What can it do? The 'stain' in this case isn't just the discolouration on the front of your coat where you leaned over the battery, or the bleached spots where you dribbled toilet cleaner on the bathroom carpet; it's the hole eaten in the fabric that really hurts. Strong acids can damage textiles, (especially nylon and other artificial fibres), metal, marble, and concrete, to say nothing of your skin.

How hard? If you catch it in time, there's hope (but not a lot). If you don't, no amount of stain-removal savvy will help, because it's **damage**, not just stain, you'll be dealing with. The key is in recognising the spill and taking quick action to neutralise it.

What to do first: Time is of the essence with acids. The minute the spill occurs, move as fast as you can. If you get acid on your clothing, the carpet, or your skin, flush with plenty of cool water immediately. This will dilute the acid so it can't do its destructive work so quickly. It also gives you time to grab something to neutralise it with. Whatever you do don't let it dry!

What to do next: *Fresh:* As soon as you've doused it with water, get a strong solution of ammonia or baking soda on the spill to neutralise the acid. Once you get the neutraliser on, you don't have to be in such a rush—it won't hurt anything now. Blot out the neutraliser solution, then rinse and blot several times with clear water. If it's a hard surface, rinse well after neutralising. If it's washable, launder it, take dry cleanables for cleaning.

Old/dry: If you've spilled acid on your clothes without realising it, you usually find out when you wash them—they emerge peppered with holes! Once the acid has dried, it's usually too late. But if you know you've spilled acid on something and it's dried, don't just throw it in the machine—the water will just activate the acid and allow it to do more dirty work. The damage may or may not already be done. Before you get the item wet, apply a neutraliser solution to stop the action of the acid, then go ahead and wash it. For dry cleanables, take the garment in and let the cleaner know about the stain, but don't count on removal.

If that doesn't do it: Wear that shirt when you're mending the car or painting the bedroom.

Caution: Stay away from strong acids—they're not only dangerous to your clothes and furnishings, but to you, too. Even weak acids like vinegar and urine can cause colour changes in some dyes and weaken cotton and linen.

Prevention: Don't wave your brush around anywhere or carry a dripping brush across the carpet when you're cleaning the toilet bowl, and don't put a wet bottle of toilet cleaner down on anything, and that includes the sink.

Adhesives (gummy adhesives—not glue or chewing gum)

What is it? The sticky substance from adhesive tape, cellophane, strapping, and other tapes, which is often left behind when the tape is removed or a plaster is walked into the carpet, etc. There's lots of adhesive, too, on those labels and stickers that are stuck somewhere on almost everything we buy.

What can it do? Stick to the surface, and get harder and more firmly bonded to it with time, heat, sunlight, and pressure. These gooey spots attract dirt and lint, too.

How hard? Fairly easy when fresh; a horribly sticky job if you leave it to dry out and harden.

What to do first: Peel off any remaining tape or sticker, and remove as much of the gummy deposit as possible. Gently scraping with a fingernail works safely on most surfaces, but on fabric be careful not to drive the adhesive deeper into the weave. Plucking it off is safer for fabrics than scraping. On hard surfaces, the adhesive can often be rolled into balls with the thumb and lifted off.

What to do next: *Fresh:* Try a proprietary grease solvent. Be careful not to rub dissolved adhesive further into fabrics. Remove the last traces of adhesive by gently rubbing and blotting with a clean cloth. Alternatively, dab with white spirit.

Old/dry: Treat as for fresh stains.

If that doesn't do it: Try Mangers De-Solv-it. If you use it on fabric, after the adhesive is gone the item should be laundered, or an oily stain will remain. Nail polish remover works well on non-plastic hard surfaces, but don't use on textiles. *Caution:* Use De-Solv-it sparingly on carpets. If you slosh it on, it'll sink down into the depths of the carpet where it's hard to get out, and keep soaking up to the surface to create a dirt-attracting, oily stain.

Prevention: Remember, it's a lot easier to apply tape than it is to get it off—pay attention to where you're putting it and don't use too much 'extra.' Pick up those stray stickers or shed plasters as soon as you see them.

Alcohol (including mixed drinks and white wine; for beer, see Beer and for red or rosé wine, see Wine)

What is it? Water, alcohol, possibly tannin, fruit, sugar, food dyes, and other additives, depending on the type of spirits and mixer.

What can it do? Alcohol can 'burn' woollen fabrics, and it oxidises and turns brown with age if left to dry on any fabric. It'll also bleed dye from many fabrics, especially artificial fibres.

How hard? Can be difficult if dried, but usually no problem if you get it while it's wet, as long as there's no dye change. Dye changes are permanent.

What to do first: Blot up all you can and sponge the spot with cool water.

What to do next: *Fresh:* Work in neat washing-up liquid along with a few drops of vinegar. Rinse. Launder washables as soon as possible in warm water. Take dry cleanables for expert spotting if any stain remains.

Old/dry: For washables, soak the garment in cool water overnight, then treat as above. For dry cleanables, rub in warm glycerine, let it sit for 30 minutes, then treat as above. Take valuable dry cleanables in for expert spotting and cleaning as soon as possible.

If that doesn't do it: Use an enzyme detergent (soak for washables, mixed to a paste with water for dry cleanables), then launder or rinse with warm water. Some alcohol stains may require treatment with a mild bleach for complete removal.

Caution: Don't iron a sugar-based stain or dry with hot air unless you're absolutely sure it's gone—heat can make it permanent.

121

Don't use soap if the drink contained fruit or fruit juice.

Prevention: Don't order anything brightly coloured or complicated on planes, trains, riverboat cruises or anywhere that you might be getting up and down a lot. Raise your Blue Hawaiian carefully and don't put the Royal Purple Punch on your best tablecloth. Bear in mind that every drink after the first one has a better chance of being spilled, slopped, dripped, or dribbled.

Anti-perspirant stains (see Perspiration)

Apple (see Fruit—Clear)

Baby Food

What is it? Vegetables, fruits, proteins, soya, synthetic compounds, usually blended with plenty of dribble.

What can it do? Some of the fruit and vegetable stains, especially, can be dark and noticeable enough to ruin clothes if allowed to set. And the combination of fruit, sugar, and other ingredients can easily be set by washing in hot water, using soap, ironing, or hot-air drying.

How hard? Usually manageable if treated while fresh. Left to dry, some of the fruit stains can become a real problem (especially the ones that end up on the ceiling!)

What to do first: Scrape off as much as you can and blot up any liquid.

What to do next: *Fresh:* For baby's clothes (washable, we hope), soak immediately in enzyme detergent for 30 minutes to an hour and then launder. For the stray spot on mum or dad's dry cleanable clothing or on carpet and upholstery, sponge with Dabitoff or The Stain Slayer, then rinse with water, feather, and air dry. If stain remains, try K2r Stain Remover Spray.

Old/dry: Washables: soak overnight in cool water and wring out. Treat the stain with laundry pre-treatment, then wash with a bleach safe for the fabric and warm water. Dry cleanables: take to dry cleaner.

If that doesn't do it: Switching babies doesn't usually do any good, but repeated launderings will often lighten or remove any remaining stains.

Caution: Don't use ammonia or other strong alkaline cleaners, or apply heat, either of which will set fruit and sugar stains.

Prevention: Don't leave half-empty baby bottles lying anywhere, and buy a bigger bib!

Ballpoint pen (see Ink—Ballpoint)

Barbecue sauce (see Tomato Ketchup and Fast Food Stains)

Beer

What is it? Water, alcohol, sugar, protein—a combination stain.

What can it do? The alcohol in beer can 'burn' woollens (turn them dark and brittle), and oxidise on any fabric to form a permanent stain; sugar stains can become permanent with heat; the protein will produce that unmistakeable stale-beer smell.

How hard? Because of the combination of ingredients, requires several steps to remove. Should be no problem if caught when fresh, but a dried-on stain can be difficult, an ironed-on one impossible.

What to do first: Don't let it dry. Blot up all you can, and sponge the spot with a mild vinegar solution, or at least with water.

What to do next: *Fresh:* After vinegar sponging, rinse with lukewarm water. Apply paste of water and enzyme detergent and let it sit for 30 minutes without drying out. Rinse in lukewarm water. Launder washables in warm water as soon as possible.

Old/dry: For washables, soak the garment in cool water overnight, then treat as above. Take dry cleanable garments for expert spotting and cleaning.

If that doesn't do it: Bleach with a mild bleach (see p. 29). If the alcohol has caused the dye to bleed or run, nothing can be done.

Caution: Don't iron a beer stain, or dry it with hot air unless you're absolutely sure it's gone–heat can make it permanent.

Prevention: Be careful when you're tipping the can to get that last drop, and remember that cans and bottles (rolling on car floors, in rubbish bins, wherever) usually contain a last little bit of beer.

Black marks on floor (see Heel Marks)

Blackberry (see Fruit—Red)

Bleach

What is it? A number of things can bleach fabrics (see p. 63). The most common cause of unwanted white or light spots on clothing and carpet is liquid chlorine bleach (such as Domestos). Whatever the cause, the treatment is the same.

What can it do? Make you a blonde, and strip the colour out of fabric and other surfaces.

How hard? The worst.

What to do first: If you get bleach on something accidentally, or notice a colour change in an item you're spotting, flood the area with cool water immediately.

What to do next: *Fresh:* Flooding it with water is all you can do. If you get it diluted quickly enough, the colour change may be slight enough to be unnoticeable. If not, it's farewell for ever.

Old/dry: Sorry. Once the dye is bleached out of a fabric, there's no way of reversing the process. Not even your tears will neutralise it. Bleached spots in carpet can sometimes be re-dyed by expert carpet dyers to more or less match the surrounding material, but there's no way you can reconstruct the pattern on your paisley blouse.

If that doesn't do it: Wear it to weed the garden, or wait until the tie-dyed look returns.

Caution: Think twice about using chlorine bleach—it isn't the wonder drug for whites we used to think it was. Most clued-up launderers use chlorine bleach only occasionally, because of its ability to weaken and deteriorate fabrics. Be very careful when storing and using chlorine bleach—make sure it's well mixed with the water before adding clothes and rinse well.

Prevention: Don't wear your favourite shirt while applying the mildew killer, and always handle bleach solutions like the dangerous liquids they are—don't splash or slosh them around.

Blood

What is it? Protein, mineral salts, water.

What can it do? Leave a faint permanent 'rust' stain if allowed to set. (Fresh bloodstains can at least get you a little sympathy and attention.)

How hard? When fresh, easy to remove. Can be a real challenge when dried and set.

What to do first: Keep the stain wet! Blot out any fresh blood, then put washables to soak in cold salt water, or rinse under the cold water tap. For dry cleanables, carpets and mattresses, sponge cold water on to the spot.

What to do next: *Fresh:* Without letting the spot dry, give washable items a cold-water wash. For dry cleanables, sponge with cold water to which you've added a few drops of ammonia, then flush thoroughly with cold water. (No ammonia on silk or wool!)

Old/dry: For washable fabrics, soak in cool salt water for several hours and rinse thoroughly. Soak again in cool water to which you've added several tablespoons of ammonia, then wash as above. For dry cleanables, sponge with salt water and treat as above.

Bloodstains often get on mattresses, pillows, upholstery, etc. Treat these according to instructions on pp. 102 and 104.

If that doesn't do it: Soak in enzyme detergent for 30 minutes to an hour, then rinse. Don't use enzyme detergents on wool or silk. If stain still remains, bleach with hydrogen peroxide and rinse. If stain still remains, use as strong a bleach as the fabric will tolerate.

Caution: Don't let the stain dry out before you've shifted it—dry blood is much more difficult to remove. Don't hot-air dry or iron until you're sure it's gone. Don't use vinegar—acids set bloodstains.

Prevention: Don't just stick a piece of loo paper over that shaving cut near your collar and hope for the best. And put a bandage on that cut finger instead of walking all over the house holding it out.

Blusher (see Make-up)

Butter (see Greasy Foods)

Candle wax (see Wax)

Carbon Paper, Typewriter/Printer Ribbon, Newsprint

What is it? Ink (dye), bonded to a ribbon, sheet, etc.

What can it do? Rub off on clothing, carpet, furniture, and hands, leaving a dark smudge.

How hard? Inked ribbons can leave a pretty tough stain; carbon paper isn't too bad; newsprint is fairly easy. If left for too long, however, the stain can become almost impossible to remove.

What to do first: If it's on your hands, wash them before touching your clothing or scratching your nose. If it's on your clothes, don't rub it! Follow the steps below and blot **gently** to avoid spreading the stain and driving it in deeper.

What to do next: *Washables:* Use a proprietary stain remover, then apply laundry pre-treatment and wash in warm water. Air dry.

Dry cleanables: Take to dry cleaner.

Hands: Thanks to the oils in skin, many inks wash off with soap and water. If it doesn't come off easily, rub in hand cleaner such as Swarfega, leave it on for a while and then wash.

If that doesn't do it: Bleach with as strong a bleach as the fabric will tolerate.

Prevention: Use plastic gloves and don't try to change ribbons while you're on the phone!

Cherry (see Fruit—Red)

Chewing Gum

What is it? Natural tree gum, sugar, colouring, flavouring.

What can it do? Stick tenaciously to carpet, hair, clothing, floors, pavements, bedposts, car doors, under tables, anywhere it lands. Then attract dirt to form a dark, ugly spot.

How hard? It's not easy, and it all depends on where, how much, and how long.

What to do first: If the gum is soft, remove as much of it as you can by gently pulling it free with your fingers. Freeze what remains with an ice cube. Small objects can just be placed in the freezer.

What to do next: *Fresh:* The moment the spot seems to be frozen stiff, give it a few quick whacks with the handle of a butter knife, while the gum is still cold and brittle. Then rub the dull edge of the knife blade briskly back and forth over the fractured glob. The gum will break up into crumbs and fall off the fabric. This works especially well on carpet, but may be too aggressive an approach for delicate fabrics. For fabrics that can't stand the knife blade treatment, just break the frozen gum with the knife handle and scrape it free with your fingernail. It's important to pick up or shake off all the little crumbs, or they'll just soften and redeposit themselves as soon as they warm up. Remove any remaining residue with Mangers De-Solv-it or The Stain Slayer. Launder. *Old/dry:* Forget trying to pull any of it off, just go directly to the freeze step and treat as above. If gum is in hair, or somewhere freezing won't work, Mangers De-Solv-it or The Stain Slayer will soften it so you can work it loose. The resulting oily spot and remaining gum residue can then be removed with Dabitoff (or shampoo, in the case of hair).

Hard surfaces: On shiny surfaces like floors, the whole glob can often be popped off with a chisel (be careful not to gouge the surface). If it's too gooey, freeze first before you start to prise.

If that doesn't do it: *Washables:* Apply laundry pre-treatment and wash in warm water. *Dry cleanables:* Take to dry cleaner.

Caution: Don't use heat of any kind, and don't iron until you're sure all traces of the stain are gone.

Prevention: Put up 'no chewing' signs. Never drop gum on floors, pavements, or out of car windows; or dispose of it anywhere without at least wrapping it in paper. Bare gum is as big a menace as bare steel.

Chocolate (sweets, cocoa, ice cream)

What is it? Fats, protein, sugar (and a habit that's hard to break).
What can it do? Make a messy brown stain that spreads easily and will oxidise and set with age and heat.
How hard? The combination of ingredients calls for a multi-method attack, but it's a fairly easy stain to remove when fresh.
What to do first: Take one last sniff, then scrape or blot up all you can, being careful not to push it deeper into the fabric. And watch where you scrape it **to**, or you'll have a second spot.
What to do next: *Fresh:* After scraping and blotting, spray with K2r Stain Remover Spray. For any remaining stain, soak washables for 30 minutes to an hour in enzyme detergent, and launder in warm water. Use paste of enzyme detergent and water on dry cleanables except for wool or silk, but don't let it dry out, then sponge-rinse with cool water.
Old/dry: Same as above, if stain has not been hot-air dried or ironed.
If that doesn't do it: *Washables:* Use a bleach safe for the fabric and launder. *Dry cleanables:* Try hydrogen peroxide. If stain is set and will not respond, take in for professional spotting.
Caution: Be sure all traces of the stain are gone before ironing or hot-air drying, as this will set it.
Prevention: Eschew chocolate mousse; make sure you've stopped shivering **before** you lift the cocoa to your lips; provided a discreet disposal container beside the chocolate box for the 'bite-and-rejects.'

Cigarette Burns

What is it? Every so often it's just nicotine and tar residues, which can be removed by spot cleaning. Usually, though, there's scorching and some charring of the fibre or surface.
What can it do? Anything from slight discolouration to a gaping hole.
How hard? The worst.
What to do first: Find out how bad it is. Is there actual damage to the fibre or surface, or just heat darkening? Remove any black or yellow-brown discolouration first, so you can assess the situation.
What to do next: *Garments:* If a hole is burned in an everyday

garment, give it up—relegate it to ragbag or work clothes. If it's an exotic, expensive, or hopelessly sentimental item, consult an expert to see if reweaving can save it. If it's just discoloured, wash it in hot water with chlorine bleach, if safe for the fabric. Sponge dry cleanables with washing-up liquid solution and rinse.

Carpet and upholstery: Camouflage is what's needed here—to blend the burn in with the surrounding area as much as possible. Lightly rub the burn with medium steel wool first. This will remove a lot of the char and lighten the colour considerably. Then vacuum up the debris. Spot clean with washing-up liquid solution and rinse.

Blackened or melted carpet tufts can be snipped off with scissors and new tufts from an out-of-the-way place glued in to fill any bald areas. After the glue is well set, brush the new tufts up straight and give them a uniform haircut. If it's a bad burn, a carpet repairer can cut the damaged section out and replace it with a piece cut from your remnants or from inside a cupboard.

About all you can do with bad burns in upholstery is replace the damaged panel or re-cover the whole piece.

Hard surfaces: Burns in wood can be spot-stripped with paint and varnish remover, sanded out, then refinished with paint or stain and varnish; or filled with suitably coloured scratch remover wax. Slight burns in plastic laminate can be removed with scouring powder, then the surface polished back to a shine with polishing compound from a car accessory shop. The same treatment will help vinyl flooring. Severe burns in plastic surfaces call for patching in a new piece or complete replacement.

Prevention: Learn to use the ash tray or give up smoking. Don't put a lighted cigarette down **anywhere** 'for a minute.' Aslett 12:14: That which is set down will be forgotten.

Cocoa (see Chocolate)

Coffee/Tea

What is it? Tannin, protein, maybe sugar and animal fat (cream or milk) or non-dairy whitener.

What can it do? A coffee spill leaves a yellowish-brown stain that can be hard to remove, especially if there was sugar in it and it has been ironed. Old, set coffee is worse.

How hard? Usually manageable when fresh, difficult if set and especially if ironed. Can be a real problem on light-coloured wool or cotton. It if had milk or cream and/or sugar, the combination of ingredients calls for a multi-method approach, and may require more than one attempt.

What to do first: Act immediately—don't let it dry out. Blot up all you can with a clean cloth, and sponge with cool water as long as any stain is coming out.

What to do next: *Washables:* Apply laundry pre-treatment and wash in warm water—air dry. For dry cleanables, smear stain with glycerine, let it sit 30 minutes, then treat as for washables. *Dry cleanables:* Sponge with a solution of water, washing-up liquid and vinegar, then flush with cool water (except for water-sensitive fabrics) and feather.

If that doesn't do it: *Washables:* soak in enzyme detergent for 30 minutes to an hour and launder in warm water and then air dry. *Dry cleanables:* apply paste of enzyme detergent and water; keep it on for 30 minutes and don't let it dry out; rinse. (Not on silk or wool.) For wool, apply glycerine, let it sit 30 minutes, and sponge off with water. Use a proprietary grease solvent to treat any stain remaining from milk or cream. Any remaining stain should be bleached with hydrogen peroxide for bleach-sensitive fabrics, or with chlorine bleach if safe (test first).

Caution: Don't use ammonia or heat—it can set a coffee stain.

Prevention: It doesn't matter **how** carefully you carry it—if you move too fast it'll slosh. Never put your cup down on the floor, even for a minute. And in case you wondered why saucers were invented, it was to catch spills and make sure there'd always be somewhere to put dripping spoons.

Cola (see Soft Drinks)

Cologne (see Perfume)

Correction Fluid (such as Tippex)

What is it? A solvent-based opaque coating (essentially, a fast-drying paint).

What can it do? Leave a highly visible spot that resists laundering.

How hard? Not too bad on fabrics that tolerate acetone. Can be hard to remove from delicate fabrics.

What to do first: Gently flake or scrape off as much as possible, being careful not to damage the fabric. Flexing the fabric before you scrape will usually help to break up the brittle coating.

What to do next: *Delicate fabrics* (acetate, triacetate, rayon, silk, and wool): Take for expert spotting and cleaning.

Durable fabrics: Sponge with nail polish remover (test first). Gently scrape or tamp to loosen the hardened film as you sponge with the solvent. When the stain is removed, flush with neutral detergent solution and rinse with water.

If that doesn't do it: Try water rinseable paint and varnish remover (test first).

Caution: Don't pluck hardened correction fluid off fabric—it can pull and tear the fibres. Flex and scrape to break up the film before trying to pull it off.

Prevention: Let it **dry**, not only before you try to write or type on it, but before you run it through the typewriter roller or lean on it. Keep the bottle close to the error so you don't have to carry a dripping brush any distance, and take the two seconds needed to wipe off brush overload before you start.

Crayons (see Wax)

Cream (see Milk)

Drain opener (see Acid)

Dye

What is it? Food colourings, hair colouring, dye transferred from dark colours in laundry. etc.

What can it do? Dyes are designed to stain, and most of them are not meant to be removed. Dyes can leave permanent stains, even when caught quickly and handled flawlessly, but often they can be removed.

How hard? The worst.

131

What to do first: Act fast—don't let it dry out. Soak washables in cool water and sponge off dry cleanables. Blot up coloured drink stains as fast as you can.

What to do next *Red:* Red is the least colourfast of all dyes—we've all had 'pink loads' where a red garment has bled colour on to a wash load of whites. This can happen with other dark colours, too. For instructions on handling this problem, see p. 33/34.

Soak washables for 30 minutes to an hour in an enzyme detergent solution. Rinse, apply laundry pre-treatment, and keep it wet 20 minutes, then launder in cool water with a bleach safe for the fabric. If colour remains, use colour remover such as Dygone Run Away or Stain Devils Colour Run Remover; test first.

For red dye stains on dry-cleanable clothing, carpets, and upholstery, the safest course is to let a professional handle it.

All other colours: Washables: Soak for 30 minutes to an hour in one quart of water to which you've added one-half teaspoon detergent and two tablespoons vinegar, substitute ammonia for vinegar if fabric is cotton or linen. Rinse, soak in enzyme detergent for 30 minutes to an hour, and launder in warm water.

Dry cleanables: Try K2r Stain Remover Spray, or sponge with Dabitoff or The Stain Slayer.

Prevention: Resist the temptation to ignore a label that tells you to wash it separately the first time. To be on the safe side, run that fuchsia tracksuit through the machine on its own the second time, too.

Egg

What is it? Protein (albumen), fats, salts, water.
What can it do? Leave you with egg on more than your face. If set by heat, can be permanent. Can also do serious damage to painted surfaces.
How hard? Easy, if caught quickly.
What to do first: Gently scrape up all you can.
What to do next: *Washables:* Soak in enzyme detergent for 30 minutes to an hour and wash in warm water. Air dry.
Dry cleanables: Apply paste of enzyme detergent and water, leave it on for 30 minutes without drying out, then rinse.
Hard surfaces: Wash it off immediately with plenty of cool washing-up liquid solution.
If that doesn't do it: Use the strongest bleach safe for the fabric.
Caution: Don't use hot water or hot-air drying—heat will set egg stains!
Prevention: Don't order soft-boiled eggs at business breakfasts. Don't carry dripping shells across the carpet.

Epoxy (see Glue—Synthetic)

Eye shadow (see Make-up)

Faeces, animal or human (see Pet Stains)

Fast Food Stains

What is it? Usually a greasy stain from a dropped french fry, a dripping burger, or a bit of dribbled soup and sandwich at lunch. Occasionally a more serious attack of Big Mac sauce or barbecue goo.
What can it do? Make you look like an idiot for the rest of the day. (If left for any length of time, can also be hard to remove.)
How hard? Ketchup and tartar sauce splotches can be a little complicated, but the simple grease spots are easy.
What to do first: If it's on the car seat, sponge it with water and leave it until you get home. If it's all down your front, get a plastic spoon and head for the Ladies. You can use a credit card if nothing else is available. Scrape off whatever you can and use loo paper to blot (don't rub!) away as much of the grease as possible. Then go to your car, handbag, or desk drawer, and get out the aerosol

stain remover such as K2r you keep handy for just such occasions. **What to do next:** *Grease spots* (meat juice, deep-fried foods, potato chips, mayonnaise, salad dressing, etc): For light stains, just spray on a little K2r, allow to dry then brush off. For heavier spots, put an absorbent pad of paper towelling behind the stain, spray K2r directly on to the spot, then sponge it through with the handkerchief. Continue until the grease is gone, then feather out the edge. (At a pinch, you can use paper towels instead of a hanky, but they'll leave the stain site clearly outlined in lint.)

Water and sugar-based stains (*soft drinks, juice, coffee, etc*): Sponge off the spot with plain cool water. If it doesn't come out entirely, fight off the urge to use soap on it—this can set fruit stains. Do the best you can with water plus washing-up liquid if available. Feather out the wet edges with a dry towel to avoid leaving a ring.

Combination stains (*hamburger sauce, barbecue sauce, etc*): Sponge first with K2r, then with cool water and a dab of soap (no soap on fruit stains). Feather the edge as you finish.

Caution: This is first aid or emergency procedure only—don't forget to take proper care of the stain when you get home by using a laundry pre-treatment, then washing. Don't hot-air dry or iron the item before the stain is gone.

Prevention: Bear in mind that takeaways have blotched a lot of garments. Don't order Big Macs when you're immaculate. Keep your hand out of the bag until you get home/to the office. Use sixteen napkins. And when scanning menus, remember that cheese glops, sauces drip and tomato slips out.

Felt-tip markers (see Ink—Felt-tip Marker)

Food colouring (see Dye)

French fries (see Fast Food Stains and Greasy Foods)

Fruit—Clear (light-coloured fruits such as apple, pear, orange, lemon, lime, grapefruit; either fresh fruit or juice)

What is it? Fruit and sugar.

What can it do? Almost invisible when fresh, clear fruit spots can turn into ugly yellowish-brown stains if you let them go, because of the sugar content.

How hard? Easy if treated when fresh; hard or impossible if set by age and heat, especially on light-coloured wool. Once a sugar stain's been ironed, it's there for life.

What to do first: Don't ignore clear fruit stains just because they don't look like much. Treat any spills immediately by first blotting up any liquid and scraping away any solids, and then sponging thoroughly with cool water.

What to do next: *Fresh: Washables:* If colour is still visible after the initial water rinse, sponge with washing-up liquid and a few drops of vinegar, then apply pre-treatment and launder. If stain still remains, soak in enzyme detergent up to an hour and launder. *Dry cleanables:* Sponge thoroughly with washing-up liquid and a few drops of vinegar, then rinse with cool water. If stain remains, apply a paste of enzyme detergent and water, let it sit for 30 minutes without drying out, then rinse with water.

Old/dry: Rub glycerine into the stain to soften it, than treat as above. If the stain has been ironed, it may be permanent.

If that doesn't do it: Bleach with as strong a bleach as the fabric will tolerate.

Caution: Don't wash in hot water. Don't use real soap—it will set fruit stains. Don't use heat, such as hot-air drying or ironing, until the stain is completely gone. Remember that fresh fruit doesn't just drip—it crunches, spurts and squirts—so don't be too quick to conclude you've got it all.

Prevention: Don't eat oranges on the new sofa. Don't wipe your hands on your apron, your best tea towel, or the back of your jeans when you're making fruit salad.

Fruit—Red (red or deeply coloured fruits such as cherry, grape, blueberry, blackberry, cranberry, or raspberry; either fresh fruit or fruit juice)

What is it? Fruit, sugar (and one of the easiest stains to see).

What can it do? Make you give up picking your own. The strong red dyes can also leave permanent stains, and the sugar will turn yellow with age and heat.

How hard? Manageable to impossible, depending on the fruit and the fabric.

What to do first: Treating it while it's still fresh is critical—the sooner the better. First scrape and blot up all you can, then immediately and repeatedly sponge with cool water until no more colour is being removed. For cotton, linen, and other sturdy white or colourfast fabrics, consider using the boiling water method below. For other fabrics, use the gentler procedures.

What to do next: *Boiling water method:* This works surprisingly well for removing fruit stains, but it must be used cautiously, and only on fresh stains. Only sturdy, colourfast fabrics (such as white or colourfast cotton and linen) that can tolerate boiling water should be considered. Pre-testing is always wise to avoid fabric damage. Stretch the stained fabric, face down, over a large bowl and secure it with a rubber band. Put the bowl in the bath, so nothing can splatter on you. Pour two pints of boiling water through the stain from a height of two to three feet. Yes, heat sets stains, but with this method the flow of hot water flushes the stain out of the fabric before it can adhere. If a stain remains after this, or if the fabric won't tolerate boiling water, go to the following procedures.

Washables: Sponge with lemon juice or rub a freshly cut lemon into the stain. Rinse with water, blot out all the moisture you can and let it air dry the rest of the way. If stain remains, sponge with washing-up liquid and a few drops of vinegar. (Dilute vinegar with two parts water for use on cotton or linen.) Tamp while sponging if the fabric will tolerate it. Apply laundry pre-treatment and launder in warm water. If the stain remains, soak in enzyme detergent for 30 minutes to an hour and relaunder.

Dry cleanables: Follow procedure for washables down through the lemon juice, washing-up liquid with vinegar, and tamping. Rinse with cool water. If stain remains, apply a paste of enzyme detergent and water, let it sit for 30 minutes without drying out, then rinse with water.

Old/dry: Rub glycerine into the stain to soften it, then treat as above. If the stain has been ironed, it may be permanent. Old stains on valuable pieces should be taken in for expert spotting.

If that doesn't do it: Bleach with as strong as bleach as the fabric will tolerate.

This is a great success if fresh

136

Caution: Don't wash in hot water. Don't use real soap—it will set fruit stains. Don't use heat (other than the boiling water method) such as hot-air drying or ironing until the stain has completely gone.

Prevention: Don't try to eat berry anything without a plate, spoon, and napkin. Don't wipe your hands on your thighs when you're picking, and watch out for juice when you're washing, hulling, cutting or transporting these tasty little morsels.

Furniture Polish

What is it? Oil; possibly dyes, waxes, or silicone.

What can it do? Dampen your enthusiasm for shiny shelves. Most polishes will make an oily stain, and the dyes in coloured polishes can leave a permanent stain. Some polishes will also alter red carpet dyes, creating a green or bluish halo around the base of polished furniture.

How hard? The darker, the more dangerous. Plain oily stains aren't too bad; dark-coloured dye stains (like dark walnut scratch cover) can be tough.

What to do first: Quickly apply an absorbent such as cat litter, talcum powder or a kitchen towel with a weight on top, and leave it on until as much of the oil as possible is absorbed. This may take several hours.

What to do next: *Fresh:* After absorbing as much oil as possible, remove the absorbent, and treat with a proprietary grease solvent. Then apply laundry pre-treatment and launder in warm water. *Old/dry:* For washables, apply laundry pre-treatment and rub in some vaseline, let it sit 15 minutes, and launder in warm water. For dry cleanables, take to dry cleaner.

If that doesn't do it: Allow the spot to dry. Sponge with washing-up liquid and a few drops of vinegar, flush with water (no vinegar on cotton or linen). If dye stains remains, treat as for Dye.

Caution: Oil stains will oxidise and become hard to remove after a few days, and even faster in the presence of heat—so treat as quickly as possible.

Prevention: Pay attention to where you're putting the polish bottle (and for that matter, your cloth). And don't get an aerosol unless you have tight control of your trigger finger.

Glue—Synthetic (superglue, epoxy resin, model-making cement, clear household adhesive, etc)

What is it? Various plastic products.

What can it do? Stick like glue to you, as well as whatever it was on originally.

How hard? Not easy when fresh; if allowed to dry, you may be stuck with it! Superglue must be treated professionally and epoxy resins cannot be removed safely when set. It's always worth asking if the manufacturer produces a solvent.

What to do first: Get it while it's still wet—don't let it dry. Gently scrape off all you can without spreading it around, and sponge the spot immediately with water to keep the glue gooey.

What to do next: *Fresh:* Although most require a solvent, soap and water remove some synthetic glues while they're still fresh. You'll probably have some glue on your hands, so wash them in soapy water to see if that shifts it. If it does, go ahead on the fabric. Acetone may be required to dissolve the clear plastic cements, but don't use acetone on acetate fabrics, and **test it first** on any fabric! Amyl acetate can be used to remove cements from acetate fabrics, but the acetone in the glue may have already damaged the fabric. Don't use acetone on plastic laminate (Formica) or vinyl. To finish up, use laundry pre-treatment on washables and launder as quickly as possible. Take dry cleanables for dry cleaning.

Old/dry: If the fabric can stand it, try soaking for half an hour in a boiling solution of vinegar and water (1:10), then launder. Water-rinseable paint and varnish remover will remove some model cements, but test first. Soaking with acetone may do it, too. To be safe, take dry cleanables in for expert spotting.

Hard surfaces: Dried glue can often be chipped off hard surfaces

(use your scraper). On porous hard surfaces like brick and concrete, you may need to use one of the spotters suggested, but test first to be sure it won't harm the surface.

If that doesn't do it: Admire it—it'll probably outlast the pyramids!

Caution: Don't try to scrape and pick dried glue from fabric—you're likely to do even more damage and distort the fibres.

Prevention: Use a piece of cardboard or a cloth behind it next time. Don't put the bottle down anywhere before putting the cap back on. Don't put the glue tube (or the dripping cap) just anywhere. Don't put on three times more than you need—it doesn't help adhesion, either.

Grape (see Fruit—Red)

Grass

What is it? Tannin, vegetable dye.

What can it do? Leave a stain that's hard to remove if set by heat or alkali (see below).

How hard? Manageable if treated when fresh.

What to do first: Sponge with plain water.

What to do next: *Washables:* Sponge with alcohol (test first). If stain remains, soak in enzyme detergent for 30 minutes to an hour, rinse thoroughly and launder in warm water with as strong a bleach as is safe for the fabric.

Dry cleanables: Sponge with alcohol (test first for colourfastness; dilute alcohol with 2 parts water for acetate fabrics; no alcohol on wool). If stain remains, sponge with vinegar, then with water. If stain remains, apply paste of enzyme detergent and water (not on wool or silk), let it sit for 15 to 30 minutes, then sponge with warm water.

If that doesn't do it: Bleach with hydrogen peroxide.

Caution: Don't use alkalis such as ammonia, degreaser, or alkaline detergent—they can set grass stains. Take care using alcohol—it can make dyes bleed. Spot-bleach dry cleanable items only as a last resort—the bleached spot may show.

Prevention: Get changed before you join the football game. Don't crouch to admire the chrysanthemums with your good trousers on. Remember that whatever you wear on a picnic will come back with these.

Gravy (see Greasy Foods)

Grease

What is it? Lubricating or 'car' grease (petroleum products); cooking grease (animal fats or vegetable oils), etc.

What can it do? Leave a semi-transparent stain that soon turns dark from all the dirt it picks up.

How hard? Fairly simple, whether fresh or old.

What to do first: Gently scrape or blot up as much as possible, without forcing it deeper into the surface. Apply an absorbent such as crushed cat litter, and let it stay on as long as needed to soak up as much of the remaining grease as possible.

What to do next: *Fresh: Washables:* Treat with laundry pretreatment, then wash in hot water.

Dry cleanables: Take to dry cleaner.

Old/dry: Forget the absorbent—it can't do much with dried grease. Rub a little Vaseline on the stain, let it sit 15 minutes, then treat as above.

If that doesn't do it: *Washables:* Try K2r Stain Remover Spray.

Caution: None

Prevention: Put on overalls or old clothes before tackling **anything** on a car. Don't grill the bacon on high. Don't fill the deep fat fryer too full. Wear an apron in the kitchen.

Greasy Foods (butter, margarine, fried foods, mayonnaise, oily salad dressings, gravy, meat juice, etc)

What is it? Animal fat or vegetable oil, along with dyes and other additives; perhaps protein and starch.

What can it do? Besides increasing your cholesterol count, most oily stains oxidise within a matter of days (faster with heat), and

the oxidation process will set any chlorinate or dye in the stain.
How hard? Fairly easy when fresh. If heated or left to oxidise, can be difficult or impossible to remove.

What to do first: If there's any solid material on the surface, such as a glob of butter or salad dressing, gently scrape up as much as possible, taking care not to drive it deeper into the fabric. For remaining oily residues, apply an absorbent and leave it on long enough to absorb as much of the oil or grease as possible (this may take several hours).

What to do next: *Fresh:* Remove absorbent. *Washables:* Treat with laundry pre-treatment and wash in hot water; air dry. *Dry cleanables:* Sponge with a proprietary grease solvent, rinse and blot dry.

Old/dry: Washables: Soak gravy, soup, mayonnaise, and other oily stains containing protein in warm enzyme detergent solution for 30 minutes to an hour. Apply laundry pre-treatment, then wash in warm water. *Dry cleanables:* Take to dry cleaner.

If that doesn't do it: If the stain is still there after washing washables, don't tumble dry or iron the object, let the fabric air dry and try K2r Stain Remover Spray.

Caution: Don't just whip out a wet cloth when you get an oily stain—water applied too soon can set it. If unsure of the contents of a food spill, read the ingredients list on the label.

Prevention: Don't try to drain the fat off mince using a fork and no lid. Shroud yourself in napkins when biting into a buttered crumpet, garlic dip, or corn on the cob. And prepare for the worst when you pour the drippings from a roasting tin to anywhere.

Hair colouring (see Dye)

Hair oil (see Lotion)

Hard-Water Stains

What is it? Minerals which are deposited on windows, bathroom fixtures, and other surfaces when hard water evaporates.

What can it do? It leaves a cloudy, scaly build-up on surfaces. It can bond semi-permanently to window glass with time and exposure to sunlight.

How hard? Not too bad if treated before it gets too thick. Hard

to remove without damaging the surface by the time the build-up is old and heavy. The hardest part of all is ignoring all the bad advice you're offered on how to get rid of it.

What to do first: Prevention is the best bet—see below.

What to do next: *Fresh:* Light, newly formed mineral scale can be wiped off hard surfaces with Ataka kettle cleaner or Jenolite paste bath cleaner. Used regularly, this will keep showers, taps and windows free of stains.

Old/heavy: Old, thick deposits can be tough. Use the same cleaners as above.

If that doesn't do it: (And it won't, if you or the chemical you apply are weak-willed), repeat above. For toilet bowls with heavy rings, a strong brick or patio cleaner from DIY store can be used.

Caution: Resist the urge to use strong chemicals such as hydrochloric acid bowl cleaners on sinks, showers, chrome taps, etc. It will take the lime scale off faster, but it'll also damage tile grout, metals, plastics, and other surfaces. Sandpaper, chisels, and dynamite are out, too, no matter how tempting.

Prevention: Rip out shower doors (they're nothing but a sliding display area for hard-water scum) and replace them with a nice, friendly inexpensive shower curtain you can just throw in the washing machine. You can also install a water softener, wipe down the shower walls before you step out, apply lemon oil after cleaning to resist build-up, adjust lawn sprinklers away from windows etc.

Heel Marks On Floors

What is it? A smear of black sole material, scuffed on to the floor as people walk over it.

What can it do? Make guests unpopular and cause family fights.

How hard? Depends on how many there are. The marks aren't

hard to remove, but if you're not careful how you go about it, you'll leave dull spots on the floor.

What to do first: Determine whether the floor has a finish (wax) on it or not—this makes a difference to how you go about things.

What to do next: *No-wax floors:* Put a dab of K2r Stain Remover Spray on the mark and rub it with a cloth. This should dissolve it. For heavy deposits, scrubbing lightly with a white nylon scourer is better and quicker. Use a clean cloth to buff the spot dry and shiny when you're done.

Waxed floors: Don't use any solvent or harsh cleaners here to soften the mark, because they'll soften and remove the wax, too. Scrub the mark lightly until it's gone with a white nylon scourer dipped in washing-up liquid solution. A good time to do this is before you do your regular mopping. If a dull area is left when it dries, buff it out with a soft cloth or apply a dab of floor finish.

Caution: Avoid the common impulse to attack these marks with steel wool pads or cleanser. You'll end up with **white** marks and scratches.

Prevention: Get rid of shoes that leave black marks, and strike black-soled guests from your list. (Or make them de-shoe at the door.)

Honey, Syrup

What is it? Sugar, water, possibly colouring.

What can it do? Besides attract flies? Leave a sticky raised spot that hardens with age and sets with heat.

How hard? Easy when fresh, only a little more difficult when old and dry, if not heat-set.

What to do first: Gently scrape to remove as much as you can

143

from the surface. Soak hardened stains with warm water before scraping. Be careful not to damage the fabric, worktop or carpet when you're scraping.

What to do next: *Washables:* Sponge with warm water until all the sticky residue has gone. Apply laundry pre-treatment and wash in warm water. Air dry.

Dry cleanables: If the fabric is water-sensitive (delicate silk, rayon, some woollens), take for expert spotting. If the fabric can tolerate a little water, sponge with warm water until all the sticky residue is gone. Sponge with washing-up liquid and a few drops of vinegar. Rinse with water and air dry.

If that doesn't do it: Soak washables in enzyme detergent for 30 minutes to an hour and relaunder. Use paste of enzyme detergent and water on dry cleanables, let sit for 30 minutes without drying out, then rinse with warm water, feather.

Caution: Don't hot-air dry or iron the item, or use hot water on it, until the stain has gone—heat sets sugar stains.

Prevention: Remember that honey jars always have syrupy sides, and watch where you put the sticky spoon.

Ice cream, chocolate (see Chocolate)

Ice Cream, Milkshakes (all flavours, except chocolate; for chocolate ice cream, see Chocolate)

What is it? Yummy enough to be worth it. Ice cream contains animal fat, sugar, food colour (dye), flavourings, maybe fruit, etc. Many milkshakes (and for that matter some ice creams) have far more smootheners, thickeners, and emulsifiers than actual dairy products in them.

What can it do? Some flavours with strong colours can leave permanent stains; sugar and fruit stains will both set hard with heat if not removed.

How hard? Vanilla and light-coloured flavours are easy if caught while fresh; raspberry ripple and its relatives can be harder.

What to do first: Put that cone down and treat the stain while fresh if possible. Scrape and blot to remove all you can, and sponge with washing-up liquid solution or at least with water, no matter where you are.

What to do next: *Fresh: Washables:* Apply laundry pre-treatment and wash in warm water. Air dry. If stain remains from flavouring, soak in enzyme detergent for 30 minutes to an hour and relaunder in warm water.

Dry cleanables: Sponge with washing-up liquid and a few drops of ammonia (no ammonia on silk or wool). Sponge-rinse with water. Air dry. If stain remains from flavouring, apply paste of enzyme detergent and water (not on silk or wool), keep moist for 30 minutes, and rinse with warm water.

Old/dry: After scraping to remove all you can, treat with a proprietary grease solvent.

If that doesn't do it: Treat as a dye stain.

Caution: Don't wash in hot water. Don't dry with heat, or iron, until stain has completely gone—heat can make sugar and fruit stains permanent.

Prevention: Don't try to eat ice cream while driving, and remember that double-scoop means double-drip!

Ink—Ballpoint Pen

What is it? One of my least favourite stains. Ballpoint ink contains various pigments and dyes in a base of solvents, oils, and resins. There are so many ink recipes around it's impossible to know which one you're dealing with—you just have to experiment. Red ink should be treated differently from all other colours (see below).

What can it do? Some ballpoint inks leave a permanent stain— cheap pens are usually the worst.

How hard? With patience and persistence, most ballpoint inks are removable, especially from synthetics. But some won't come out, especially from cotton and wool, for anything short of scissors.

What to do first: Treat it as soon as possible—it's much easier

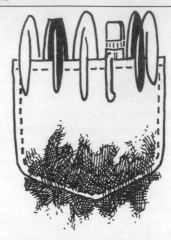

when fresh. If you can identify the offending pen, put a smudge of ink on a scrap of similar fabric and test to see which of the following procedures works best.

What to do next: *Washables:* Sponge with water and washing-up liquid. If colour transfers to your sponging cloth, keep sponging with water until no more colour is coming out. Blot dry. Saturate the stain with cheap hair spray and blot it through into a fresh cloth—continue until no more colour is being transferred. Apply laundry pre-treatment and wash in warm water; air dry. This will remove most ballpoint ink stains. (Some laundry stain removal sticks work well on some inks, in place of the hair spray and pre-treatment.)

Dry cleanables: For an expensive garment, especially silk, wool, rayon, or acetate, the safest course is to take it for professional spotting and cleaning. If you're feeling extra brave, or it's a garment you're not deeply attached to, try the procedures for washable garments, but instead of washing, just rinse with warm water and air dry.

If that doesn't do it: If stain remains after washing, air dry—don't use heat. Try the following solvents one after the other (pre-test first!) until you find one that removes the ink; then sponge the stain with it until no more colour comes out: surgical spirit, acetone (don't use acetone on acetate), amyl acetate. If stain remains, use hydrogen peroxide or a bleach safe for the fabric. If a yellow stain remains, treat as a rust stain.

Caution: All of these spotting agents can be hazardous—either to you or to what you're working on. Follow all label directions and safety precautions, and don't fail to pre-test the fabric in a hidden place.

For red ink: Sponge with washing-up liquid and ammonia (where safe) until colour is no longer removed. Rinse, then treat with surgical spirit and vinegar. Rinse again, and treat any remaining stain with hydrogen peroxide. Rinse well.

Prevention: Beware of pens that have been sticking tip-down in penholders or desktop mugs for longer than anyone can remember. Do clean off pen tips when they get clogged, but resist the impulse to do it with your fingers. Click it—or cap it—before you put it in your pocket.

Ink—Felt-tip Markers

What is it? Dye and solvents.

What can it do? Decorate your cuff, wall, or tablecloth, or live up to that 'permanent' on the label.

How hard? There are two kinds of markers: permanent and non-permanent ('washable'). Most permanent marker stains will not come out completely. The non-permanent type can usually be removed, but some take more work than others.

What to do first: Try to identify the culprit—it helps a lot to know which type you're dealing with. If the stained item is expensive, or one you hate to lose, take it for professional spotting. There's no guarantee it'll come out, but the chances are better in the hands of a pro. If you don't know what the marker was, first try the non-permanent procedure, then the permanent one if the stain remains.

What to do next: *Non-permanent:* For dry cleanable items, especially expensive garments or delicate fabrics, the best bet is professional spotting and dry cleaning. For washables (or dry cleanables you're willing to risk), try this: sponge the stain with methylated spirit being careful not to spread it. Continue until no more colour is being removed. For washables, apply laundry pre-treatment along with a few drops of ammonia, and launder garment in warm water. For carpet, upholstery, and nonwashable fabrics, apply laundry pre-treatment and ammonia, tamp, then rinse with warm water.

Permanent: Don't get your hopes up, but the following procedures will sometimes remove permanent marker stains, and will

147

almost always lighten them somewhat: sponge the stain repeatedly with correction fluid solvent, obtainable at an office supply store. **If that doesn't do it:** Sponge with surgical spirit (test first). If stain remains, bleach with hydrogen peroxide. And remember this at Christmas when you're tempted to buy a set for your nephews and nieces.

Caution: When you first start on a marker stain, be very careful not to spread it. There's a lot of strong dye there, and it'll go a long way. Use a spotter sparingly and blot gently, keeping the wetted area as small as you can.

Prevention: Remember that the soft tip of a felt-tip pen can not only stain but keep on drawing out ink, and staining, until the whole marker is empty. So think CAP! before you plunge it into your pocket, bag, or briefcase. Don't put uncapped markers down anywhere, and remember that markers with square or hexagonal sides are far less likely to roll away.

Ink—Indian

What is it? Carbon or 'lamp' black in a shellac or gelatine base.
What can it do? If it dries, you're guaranteed a permanent stain.
How hard? Possible to remove from some surfaces if caught immediately. Once it's dry, it can rarely be completely removed.
What to do first (after wishing you'd picked a more forgiving medium): **Immediately** flush the fabric with plenty of cool water, until as much pigment as possible has been removed.
What to do next: *Fresh:* After flushing with water, sponge with ammonia and rinse (dilute ammonia 1:1 with water for silk or wool; if ammonia causes colour change in any fabric, apply vinegar and rinse). For washables, apply laundry pre-treatment and launder in warm water. Take dry cleanables in for expert spotting and cleaning.
Old/dry: Washables: Soak overnight in a solution of 4 tablespoons ammonia to two pints water, apply laundry pre-treatment and launder in warm water. *Dry cleanables:* If the piece is valuable, take it in for expert spotting, but don't expect a miracle.
If that doesn't do it: Forget it. Bleach won't alter carbon stains.
Prevention: Keep permanent inks out of reach of children, and put on old clothes or an apron before using them. Don't plunge your pen or brush in too deep, and refill the bottle before it drops down below half.

Jam

What is it? Fruit, sugar.

What can it do? If you leave it, the sugar will turn yellow with age and heat. There may also be staining from the natural dyes in the fruit.

How hard? Spots from light-coloured jams and jellies are easy to remove if not set by heat or soap. Some of the red or purple jam stains can be perplexing.

What to do first: Scrape to remove as much as possible, and sponge with warm water.

What to do next: *Washables:* Apply laundry pre-treatment, then sponge thoroughly with water to remove sugar residue. If stain remains, treat as for Fruit. If the spot seems to be gone, wash in warm water.

Dry cleanables: Sponge thoroughly with warm water to remove sugar residue. If stain remains, treat as for Fruit. Don't forget to feather the edges.

Old/dry: Apply glycerine to soften the stain, let it sit 30 minutes, and rinse with warm water. Treat as above. Last traces may be removed with hydrogen peroxide. If the stain has been ironed, it may be permanent.

Caution: Don't tumble dry, or iron the item, or use hot water on it, until the stain has gone—heat will set it. Don't use soap—it sets fruit stains.

Prevention: Stop spreading an inch before the edge of the bread. Don't serve jam doughnuts to anyone under twenty-one.

Lemon (see Fruit–Clear)

Lime (see Fruit—Clear)

Lipstick, Shoe Polish (paste, not liquid)

What is it? Dye in an oil-soluble wax base.

What can it do? Leave an intensely coloured stain that can be easily spread, and tends to set with heat and age.

How hard? Tough, even when handled immdiately. Can be impossible to remove completely if old and set.

What to do first: Gently pluck and scrape to remove as much solid material from the surface as possible. Be careful not to spread the stain or force it in deeper. Don't use water, solvents, or heat at first—these will only spread and set the stain.

What to do next: *Fresh:* Blot with nail polish remover (not on acetates). Change your cloth often to carry away dissolved dye. Change sponge pads as needed, too, to avoid redepositing dissolved colour. Be careful not to spread the stain. Sponge remaining dye stain with washing-up liquid and a few drops of ammonia, tamping if fabric will tolerate it (no ammonia on silk or wool). Apply laundry pre-treatment and launder washables in hot water. Rinse dry cleanables with warm water.

Old/dry: Apply glycerine and allow to sit 30 minutes to soften stain, then treat as above.

If that doesn't do it: Sponge with methylated spirit (test first) and rinse with water. Use household bleach on any remaining stain, if fabric will tolerate it (test first). Professional spotting or colour stripping may be required.

Caution: A little of this stuff goes a long way, so take extra care to remove as much solid matter as possible before applying solvent. There's a lot of dye in even a tiny particle of these things, so remove as much as you can before starting to dissolve it. If it's a valuable piece, the best bet is to take it for expert spotting. Ditto if you get a 'lipstick load' of stained garments from washing something with a lipstick left in a pocket.

Prevention: Stop pretending that you'll ever polish a shoe without dropping black or burgundy globs somewhere. Put down old newspapers before you begin. And as for lipstick, if you really love him (or have to do his laundry), don't apply a fresh coat just before he walks through the door.

Lotion (hand, lotion, body lotion, suntan lotion, hair oil)

What is it? Mineral or vegetable oil, glycerine, moisturisers, perfume, dye.

What can it do? Leave an oil slick that attracts dirt—the darkened, dirty areas on the arms and headrest of upholstered chairs are typical.

How hard? Comes off most things easily when fresh; oxidises and hardens with age.

What to do first: For fresh spills or heavy deposits, apply an absorbent such as cat litter and leave on for several hours to blot up the excess oil. Shake or brush off when dry.

What to do next: *Carpet and upholstery:* Apply a proprietary grease solvent, tamp, and blot. Continue until the stain is gone. Sponge with water, rinse and blot.

Washables: Apply laundry pre-treatment, then smear the spot with Vaseline and wash in hot water.

Dry cleanables: Take to dry cleaner.

Old/dry: Apply glycerine or Vaseline to soften the stain, then treat as above.

If that doesn't do it: Sponge with washing-up liquid and a few drops of ammonia (no ammonia on silk or wool). Rinse with water.

Prevention: This stuff is so soothing we tend to lavish it on double thick and splash it everywhere. Go easy, and give it a chance to be absorbed before you leave the bathroom or lower yourself on to the lounger.

Make-up (liquid foundation, mascara, blusher, eye shadow, etc)

What is it? Dye in various wax and oil-base creams, emulsions, and powders.

What can it do? Leave a colourful stain that's easy to spread.

How hard? Usually removable, but can be as hard as making ourselves look beautiful some days, particularly if set by heat.

What to do first: Gently brush or scrape to remove as much solid material from the surface as possible, being careful not to force the stain in deeper.

What to do next: *Fresh:* Sponge with a proprietary grease solvent, then wash in warm water. Take dry cleanables to the cleaners.

Old/dry: Take to dry cleaner.

If that doesn't do it: Take to dry cleaner.

Caution: With potent stainmakers like these, take extra care to remove as much as possible before applying solvent. If it's a valuable piece, the best bet is to take it for expert spotting.

Prevention: Washing your face before bed is kinder to complexions as well as pillowcases. And make sure that bottles and compacts are securely closed before you pop them into your bag or pocket.

Margarine (see Greasy Foods)

Mascara (see Make-up)

Mayonnaise (see Greasy Foods)

Meat juice (see Greasy Foods)

Mildew

What is it? A tiny live plant—a fungus.

What can it do? Make the bathroom and a lot of other places highly unromantic. Mildew leaves black, grey, orange, blue, or white specks or splotches on the surface of whatever it's growing on, and will gradually digest and destroy organic materials like cloth, paper, and wood.

How hard? One of the worst, since it isn't just a stain, it's actually a menace to the material it's on. If a jute-backed carpet gets flooded, mildew can eat away half the strength of the backing in just a few days. And mildew is **alive**, so it can multiply!

What to do first: Kill it, so that it can't do any more damage. Mildew thrives in dark, damp, warm, poorly ventilated conditions. Just putting the object out in the sunlight or drying it out will slow mildew growth dramatically.

What to do next: *Hard surfaces:* For bleach-safe surfaces such as tiled bath and shower surrounds and painted walls, use a 1:5 solution of liquid household bleach in cool water. Apply and scrub with a stiff nylon scrubbing brush, then rinse. This not only kills the mildew, but bleaches out the stains in the grout. Mildew killer, sold in DIY stores, is also very effective.

Garments: Washables: Brush off as much mildew as you can, wash the garment with household bleach if the fabric and colour can tolerate it. Mildew stains are so sinister, you should consider using bleach even on garments where you'd normally avoid it. Just be sure to test first for colourfastness. *Dry cleanables:* Take immediately for professional cleaning.

Leather: (Finished leather): Take the mildewed article outside if possible and gently brush all the surface specks away. Sponge with a mild solution of disinfectant. Polish with a good quality leather polish. *Carpeting:* When jute-backed carpet gets wet, it's important to dry it out as quickly as possible. Steam cleaning isn't enough. The carpet needs either to be taken up and dried, or dried in place with special fans that balloon the carpet up and blow air underneath. Your local carpet cleaner is the expert who will know how to do all this. Ideally, the back of the carpet should also be treated with a mildewcide

If that doesn't do it: You might consider moving to the Sahara.

Caution: When working with household bleach, remember not to mix it with any other cleaning compounds except detergent. Combining it with strong acids or alkalis (ammonia, degreaser, caustic soda) can produce deadly gases.

Prevention: Don't put **anything** away wet.

Milk (cream)

What is it? Animal fat, albumen, water.

What can it do? Set and start to smell if not removed.

How hard? Simple if caught when fresh. Hard it heat-set.

What to do first: Don't wait. Blot up all you can immediately with a dry cloth.

What to do next: *Fresh: Washables:* Sponge with cool water. Apply laundry pre-treatment and let it sit for a few minutes, then launder in cool water. Air dry. If stain remains, soak in enzyme detergent for 30 minutes to an hour and wash again.

Dry cleanables: Sponge with washing-up liquid solution and a few drops of ammonia (no ammonia on silk or wool - use borax instead), then with cool water. If stain remains, apply paste of enzyme detergent and water (not on silk or wool), let it sit for 30 minutes without drying out, then rinse. Don't forget to feather edges with each step.

Old/dry: Treat as above.

If that doesn't do it: Treat with as strong a bleach as the fabric will tolerate.

Prevention: Keep the bucket away from the cow's back legs, and count on the cat sticking her head in the saucer just as you start to pour.

Mud (dirt)

What is it? Soil and water.

What can it do? Make you look as if you're fresh from a rugby scrum. And if you scrub while it's wet, it'll spread and get embedded.

How hard? Usually easy to remove, except for strongly coloured earth.

What to do first: Let it dry. Then dry-brush or vacuum away as much as possible before wetting the stain. You can get rid of 90 per cent of most mud stains this way.

What to do next: *Washables:* Apply laundry pre-treatment and

wash in warm water. This will remove all but the toughest mud stains.

Dry cleanables: Sponge with washing-up liquid solution, then rinse with water. If stain remains, sponge with a few drops of vinegar. Rinse, feather, and air dry.

If that doesn't do it: Deeply coloured mud may need additional work. A soak in enzyme detergent for 30 minutes to an hour (use a paste of detergent and water on dry cleanables) may help. Red earth stains will sometimes respond to rust remover but test first (see p. 166).

Prevention: Get rid of bare dirt in the garden and switch to smooth-soled shoes!

Mustard

What is it? Turmeric, a bright yellow spice, is what does the staining.

What can it do? Put you in a mood that's anything but mellow yellow. If mustard is allowed to set, it can be impossible to remove.

How hard? Not easy when fresh, and extremely difficult when set by heat or alkali (ammonia, etc).

What to do first: Scrape and blot to remove all you can then treat **immediately.**

What to do next: *Fresh:* For washables, apply glycerine followed by a few drops of vinegar, then wash in cool water. For dry cleanables, sponge with washing-up liquid and a few drops of vinegar, rinse with cool water.

Old/dry: Scrape away as much of the dried crust as possible, flexing the fabric to break embedded residue. Apply glycerine and let it sit for 30 minutes, then treat as above.

If that doesn't do it: Bleach with hydrogen peroxide.

Caution: Don't use ammonia or heat—both will set mustard stains.

Prevention: Don't eat hot dogs en route, and remember that the spoon is steadier that the squirter. (And as every street vendor knows, wrapping a napkin around your 'dog' is the best way to prevent mustard stains.)

Mystery Stain

What is it? If we knew, it wouldn't be a mystery.

What can it do? Make you very nervous, especially if it's on something expensive. (Perhaps it's contagious.)

How hard? We'll hope it's something easy until we're proven wrong.

What to do first: See opposite. If that doesn't shed any light on it, blot or scrape to remove all you can.

What to do next: For unknown stains, start with a proprietary grease solvent and rinse with water—that's the safe way. If that doesn't remove it, try the following chemicals in order, until you find something that softens or loosens the stain. Once you find something that works, stay with it until no more colour is coming out. Tamp or scrape if the fabric will tolerate it. Go to the next chemical only if a stain remains. When the stain is gone, flush or rinse as indicated, and let it air dry.

Six Clues for Stain Detectives

If you know what a stain is when you start working on it, the chances of removal are about doubled. What do you do when you run up against a mystery stain?

1. Colour is a real clue. But remember, as things dry they often change colour. Fresh sugar stains are usually light-coloured, but old, caramelised sugar is yellow-brown. Brightly coloured stains like blood and tomato turn duller and darker as they set. Fruit, grass and ink don't change much in colour as they dry. Paint, glue and nail polish hardly change at all.

2. The **look and feel** of a stain often provide a clue. Is it oily or dry? Opaque or transparent? Built-up and crusty, or with no solid material at all on the surface? Is it brittle or sticky? Hard or soft? Shiny or dull? Is it all one colour or texture, or does it seem to be a mixture? Thinking about how something looks and feels when it dries will often help solve your mystery. Dried mustard and dried honey look similar, but the honey will feel stiff, the mustard much softer.

3. It's a safe guess that **sticky, gooey stains are sugar-based.** Most dried sugar stains will turn white when scratched.

4. Is it an **oil stain?** A lot of stains are oily, and oily stains go dark. A grease stain set by laundering is usually dark brown. Oily stains look alike after they've picked up dirt. It may have started out as mayonnaise, margarine or motor oil, but they all look much the same after they've been walked on for a while. If a dried stain is still soft and flexible, is dark and dirty in colour and is soaked into the surface rather than raised, it's probably a grease or oil stain.

5. Alcohol, beer, perfume, and many food stains can be identified by their **smell**—so scratch and sniff!

6. Circumstantial evidence can also help you to pin it down. How big is the spot? Where is it on the chair or cardigan? Is it a single drop, or a dribble or spray? Might there be an imprint along with the stain, to help reveal what you rubbed or leaned against? What **room** is the injured object in, and what kind of activities take place there? Where was the stained piece last, and what was served or used there? The marks on your son's sports clothes might mystify you, until you learn that he recently won the mud-wrestling contest.

Amyl acetate—flush
Cool water—blot
Washing-up liquid with a few drops of **vinegar** (no vinegar on cotton or linen)—rinse with water
Washing-up liquid with a few drops of **ammonia** (no ammonia on silk or wool-use borax instead)—rinse with water
Bleach—the strongest bleach safe for the fabric
If that doesn't do it: Take it for professional cleaning (but make sure you confess to your own unsuccessful attempts to date).
Caution: For an unknown spot on something valuable, taking it immediately for professional spotting and cleaning is unquestionably the best approach.
Prevention: If you treat it as soon as it happens, while you still remember what it is, you're much less likely to have mystery stains.

Nail Polish

What is it? A very fast-drying enamel or lacquer.
What can it do? Bond to fibres as it hardens, leaving a stiff raised spot. And the dyes in nail varnish can cause permanent stains.
How hard? One of the worst, even if you tackle it immediately.
What to do first: Act fast—nail varnishes are designed to dry almost instantly! Blot or gently scrape as much as possible out of the fabric, them immediately apply the proper solvent (see below) to keep the spot from drying out.
What to do next: *Fresh:* For acetate, triacetate, modacrylic, rayon, silk, and wool, apply glycerine and take the garment to a dry cleaner immediately for professional spotting. For other fabrics, dab acetone or non-oily nail varnish remover on an inconspicuous place to test for colourfastness. If the colour doesn't change, and there's no fabric damage, flush the stain repeatedly with acetone or polish remover until no more colour is being removed. Tamp as necessary to help loosen the stain. Launder. Air dry. If acetone damages the dye or fabric, use amyl acetate instead.
Old/dry: Soak the stain with amyl acetate to soften it, then treat as above.
If that doesn't do it: Sponge with alcohol (test first). Bleach with as strong a bleach as the fabric will tolerate. Try colour remover as a last resort.
Caution: When using acetone, be sure to pre-test first, and protect

your work area—acetone softens paint, varnish, and plastics. Keep acetone away from sparks or flame, and use only in a well-ventilated area. Don't use acetone on acetate, triacetate, or modacrylic fabrics.

If that doesn't do it: Snip off the Crushed Cranberry part and turn the rest into dusters.

Prevention: Don't put the bottle—even for a second—on the sofa arm, the carpet, or the back of the wicker elephant. Don't balance the bottle between your knees, or on your thigh. Instead, make it a habit to put it on a firm flat surface covered with a disposable cloth.

Newspaper ink (see Carbon Paper)

Oil (car, cooking, lubricating)

What is it? Vegetable, animal, or petroleum (mineral) oil.

What can it do? Leaves a dark penetrating stain that attracts other soil and dirt.

How hard? Fairly simple if not allowed to set and as long as you're not captain of an oil tanker.

What to do first: Gently scrape or blot up as much as possible, without forcing the stain deeper into the fabric. For fresh stains, apply an absorbent such as cat litter, weight it down, and let it stay on long enough to soak up as much of the oil as possible.

What to do next: *Fresh: Washables:* Treat with laundry pre-treatment then wash in water as hot as the fabric will stand.

Dry cleanables: Take to dry cleaner.

Old/dry: Take to dry cleaner.

If that doesn't do it: Take to dry cleaner.

Prevention: If you're man or woman enough to change the oil in your car, you can be careful where you put your jeans when you come in the house.

Orange (see Fruit—Clear)

Oven Cleaner

What is it? Usually caustic soda.

What can it do? Not only eat your skin, but rapidly damage silk and wool, and leave white spots on coloured fabrics. It can also injure some paints and varnishes.

How hard? Easy if you get it off fast before any damage is done. If not, forget it!

What to do first: Act quickly, especially if spilled on silk, wool, skin, or paint. Scrape to remove all you can (be careful what you do with this corrosive material afterwards), and flush immediately with cool water.

What to do next: *Fresh:* Neutralise it with vinegar, then rinse with cool water.

Old/dry: Soak with mild vinegar solution for a few minutes to neutralise, and rinse with cool water. If damage has been done, it can't be reversed.

Prevention: Don't wear anything you're fond of when working with oven cleaner, and do wear rubber gloves and long sleeves. Protect the surroundings well with old papers and use a brush or cloth to apply to tricky spots like the door frame and the edges of the door. No one can aim an aerosol well enough to avoid hitting at least two innocent bystanding surfaces.

Paint—Oil-based (gloss)

What is it? Pigments, resins, solvents, oil.

What can it do? Get on to anything you don't want it to, always in a contrasting colour. Then it dries to a hard raised spot that bonds tightly to the fabric and can be impossible to remove.

How hard? A hassle even when wet, depending on the pigments; very difficult when dry.

What to do first: Don't let it dry! Blot out as much as possible with a paper towel or cloth.

What to do next: *Fresh:* Flush with turps or paint brush cleaner. Tamp if needed to loosen the spot. If you can't flush solvent through the fabric (upholstered furniture, carpet, etc.), apply it repeatedly and blot it out each time until all paint colour is removed.

Old/dry: Take to dry cleaner.

Hard surfaces: The easiest solution is to wipe up spatters while they're still wet. Dried specks can be removed from glass and ceramic tile with a glass scraper (wet the surface first): from aluminium trim and other metals with cellulose thinner, but be careful on Formica, enamelled appliances, and vinyl flooring—it can soften the finish if it sits for too long. For surfaces that won't stand thinner or scraping, wet with turps or white spirit and scrape gently with a plastic or nylon scraper. Specks on your watch, glasses, and other such delicates are best removed with that exquisitely tuned instrument, the human fingernail. It's hard enough to really work, yet soft enough to not scratch most surfaces, and it's controlled by the world's most sensitive computer. Wetting the surface with the appropriate solvent before any scraping not only lubricates the surface to help prevent scratches, but also softens the paint and makes removal easier.

If that doesn't do it: *Washables:* Apply laundry pre-treatment and wash in warm water—air dry. *Dry cleanables:* Apply laundry pre-treatment and sponge with cool water—if stain remains, take for expert spotting. *On carpet:* You can use pliers to pinch and pulverise dry drops, then vacuum them up.

Caution: The safest course for a dried-out paint stain on an expensive object is to take it for expert spotting.

Prevention: Don't dip your brush in up to the knuckles, and try to find a safe place to put the lid. Or go away for the weekend while a painter does the whole job.

Paint—Water-Based (emulsion, acrylic, water-based exterior gloss)

What is it? Water, polymer resins, pigments.
What can it do? Dry to a tough, raised, highly visible spot.
How hard? Fairly easy when fresh because emulsion dissolves in water; can be difficult once it starts to dry. Cures become harder and harder over a period of days. Some water-based paints, especially acrylics, are impossible to remove once they've dried.
What to do first: Gently blot up all you can with a paper towel, being careful not to drive the paint deeper into the surface. Wet the stain with water immediately to prevent it from drying out.
What to do next: *Fresh:* Sponge with warm washing-up liquid solution, continuing until no more paint is being removed. For washables, apply laundry pre-treatment and wash immediately in warm water, then air dry. For dry cleanables and carpet, sponge with washing-up liquid, tamping as needed to loosen any partially dry areas, flush with water, then air dry. For large spills of paint on carpeting, flood the area with water and blot out with towels or a wet/dry vacuum. Continue until no more paint is being removed, then treat as above. Alternatively, seek professional advice.
Old/dry: Take to dry cleaner.
Hard surfaces: See Paint—Oil-Based
If that doesn't do it: Spray with K2r Stain Remover Spray.
Caution: If you have a dried-out paint stain on an expensive object, the safest course is to take it for expert spotting.
Prevention: Wipe surrounding woodwork/floor/whatever with a damp cloth a soon as you finish painting an area, to catch specks and spatters while they're still wet and easy to remove.

Peanut butter (see Greasy Foods)

Pear (see Fruit—Clear)

Pencil Lead, Indelible Pencil

What is it? Graphite.
What can it do? Give you black marks, and leave a streak of embedded graphite particles.
How hard? Fairly easy on synthetics, can be tricky on white cotton

or linen, not a problem on most hard surfaces.

What to do first: Vacuum or shake out any loose particles.

What to do next: *Washables:* Use a soft, kneadable art gum eraser or a blob of dried Cow Gum to gently blot and wipe out the mark. A soft pencil rubber works, too, but not as well. Be careful not to distort the fabric. Apply laundry pre-treatment, along with a few drops of ammonia, and wash immediately in warm water.

Dry cleanables: Erase stain as above. If stain remains, sponge with washing-up liquid and a few drops of ammonia. Rinse with warm water and feather.

Hard surfaces: Pencil will wipe off non-porous surfaces like enamel paint and Formica with a washing-up liquid solution. For porous surfaces like raw wood, wallpaper, and emulsion paint, erase with an art gum eraser as above.

If that doesn't do it: Repeat above. For indelible pencil, sponge with surgical spirit (test first for colour fastness; dilute with two parts water for use on acetate; do not use alcohol on silk or wool).

Prevention: Empty the pencil sharpener before it's over-full, and remember to retract the lead in your propelling pencil before you jam it into your shirt pocket.

Perfume, Cologne

What is it? Alcohol, essential oils, fragrances.

What can it do? Like any alcohol stain, perfume can burn wool, and will eventually oxidise and turn brown on any fabric. The alcohol in perfume or cologne can also cause dye to bleed in some fabrics.

How hard? Not usually a problem if treated when fresh. If left to dry or if dye bleeds, it can be impossible.

What to do first: Treat immediately, while still wet. Blot up all you can and sponge the spot with cool water.

What to do next: *Washables:* Apply laundry pre-treatment and wash in warm water. If stain remains, treat as for dry cleanables.

Dry cleanables: Blot out as much of the water as you can and apply warm glycerine; tamp if the fabric will allow it. Rinse with cool water. If any stain remains, sponge with mild vinegar solution, then rinse with cool water. Blot as dry as possible and feather the edges.

Old/dry: Take for expert spotting and cleaning.

If that doesn't do it: Sponge with surgical spirit (test first for

163

colour fastness; dilute with two parts water for use on acetate;
don't use alcohol on silk or wool).

Prevention: Don't squirt dead centre of a low-necked dress, even
if the movie heroines always did. You may end up with a stain in
the worst imaginable location. Go for the pulse points like wrists
and behind the ears and knees, where perfume has the most
powerful effect anyway. And get rid of those dark, rancid bottles
littering the dressing table—they're the worst offenders.

Perspiration

What is it? Body oils, mineral salts, enzymes.

What can it do? Not only make you unpopular, but weaken and
discolour fabric if not removed.

How hard? Usually no sweat, unless heat-set. Some anti-
perspirants combine with sweat to make the stain more tenacious.

What to do first: *Washables:* Soak for 30 minutes to an hour in
enzyme detergent, then wash in warm water. If stain has
discoloured fabric, use as strong a bleach as is safe for the fabric.
Dry cleanables: Sponge with washing-up liquid and a few drops of
ammonia (no ammonia on silk or wool). Flush with water and
feather.

If stain or odour remains: Soak washables in vinegar solution,
then wash again.

Caution: Never iron anything with untreated perspiration
stains—the heat will set them.

Prevention: Wear absorbent underwear such as cotton rather than synthetics to at least help prevent. And if sweat stains are a real problem for you, or you have a truly elegant garment you want to protect, there are such things as underarm shields. (Be careful which brightly coloured tops you wear under white jackets—or you'll have a dye stain blended with the sweat stains.)

Pet Stains (Urine and faeces)

Since pet stains on carpet are the big problem, the following concentrates on carpet. For pet (and human) waste stains on upholstery and bedding, use the same process, but see p. 000 to adapt it to those surfaces.

What is it? Protein, urea, organic waste, zillions of bacteria.

What can it do? They may be more vile-smelling and repelling, but faeces are easier to remove and much less of a threat than urine. If urine penetrates into the carpet backing and underlay and isn't completely removed while fresh, you're in trouble. Urine changes chemically as it dries and ages, and you can end up with permanent yellow stains and a very persistent residual odour.

How hard? If you handle them properly at once, pet stains can be removed completely. Put off or ignored, they become extremely difficult to impossible. Plus they'll encourage Fido or Felix to give you a repeat performance in the same place!

What to do first: Scrape up any solid matter, being careful not to force it deeper into the pile. Blot up any free liquid by putting a folded towel or absorbent pad over the spot (resist the urge to use Fluffy himself) and pressing gently with your foot. Go easy at first so as not to force urine deeper into the carpet. Keep changing the towel and applying increased foot pressure until no more moisture is being transferred to the towel. Finish by putting your whole weight on the towel, to sop up every last bit of liquid possible.

What to do next: *Fresh:* After scraping and blotting thoroughly, apply a pet stain remover such as Shaws No-Stain.

Old/dry: If you have carpet riddled with old, dried urine stains that smell terrible even after steam cleaning, call in an odour control specialist. The cure will probably involve removing the carpet, sealing the floor, replacing the underlay, cleaning and deodorising the carpet both front and back, and reinstalling it.

If that doesn't do it: Replace the carpet, put a potted palm over the spot, or consider switching to hermit crabs.

Caution: Don't believe the advertising for miracle pet stain removers that 'You just spray on and wipe off and the stain disappears like magic!' Anything that works permanently has to get down to the source of the odour and eliminate it. Urine odours treated with quick fixes will be back to haunt you!

Never use ammonia on pet accident sites—its urine-like odour will actually *attract* pets.

Prevention: Don't **create** a pet that's accident prone—spend the little bit of time it takes to make sure that the new puppy is 100 per cent house trained (it'll save lots of cleaning and cursing later). Don't let the cat tray get so gross that no self-respecting cat would use it, and don't stuff your pet with people food.

Plant food (see Chemical Stains, p. 62)

Polyurethane (see Paint—Oil-Based)

Potato crisps (see Fast Food Stains and Greasy Foods)

Printer ribbon (see Carbon Paper)

Raspberry (see Fruit—Red)

Rust

What is it? Iron oxide. Rust stains get on to fabrics and other surfaces from contact with wet iron or steel. Little brown spots on your clothing are probably rust, either from a worn washing machine or dryer drum, or from iron in your water supply. Household bleach makes dissolved iron precipitate out of water, causing rust stains in the wash. A rust-coloured stain on plumbing fixtures is caused by iron in the water, too.

What can it do? Leave a reddish-brown spot that bonds tightly to the surface.

How hard? Comes off like magic from fabrics treatable with proprietary rust remover; can be very difficult on delicate fabrics that must be dry cleaned.

What to do next: *Washables:* The quickest and easiest treatment is with a cleaner such as Jenolite rust killing solution. Handle with care, though.

A fairly reliable home remedy is to apply salt to the stain, then drip on lemon juice. Hold it over steam or let it dry in the sun, then rinse. Repeat as necessary. A lot slower, but safer.

Delicate fabrics (silk, wool, fibreglass, metallic fabrics, acetate, rayon): These fabrics can't handle proprietary rust removers. Take them for expert spotting.

Bathroom fixtures: For rust stains in sinks and tubs, use Jenolite Bath Stain Remover.

Caution: Don't ever use household bleach—it actually sets rust stains.

Prevention: If you have iron-rich water, leave bleach out of the laundry. Get rid of that old tumble dryer with the rusty drum.

Salad dressing (see Greasy Foods)

Scorch

What is it? A burn, usually from a hot iron. If it's dark, it's probably burned fibre. If it's light, this could be your lucky day, perhaps it's only burned starch or soap residue, which will wash out.

What can it do? Leave a mark on the fabric, ranging from faint tan to dark brown, as well as damage it.

How hard? Light scorch can usually be removed or lightened considerably. Dark scorch is probably permanent—it's particularly difficult to remove from silk and wool.

What to do first: Be aware that if the fibres are significantly scorched, they'll be weakened, and anything you do may cause

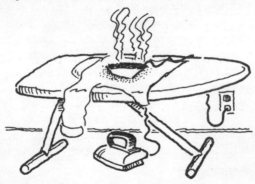

further damage (but what have you got to lose?).

What to do next: *Washables:* Apply laundry pre-treatment or liquid detergent to the stain and wash in hot water. Or sponge with hydrogen peroxide and a few drops of ammonia before washing.

Dry cleanables: Sponge with a hydrogen peroxide and a few drops of ammonia. Rinse with cool water and blot dry; feather the wet edge. If a stain remains, you can try professional dry cleaning, but don't expect a miracle.

If that doesn't do it: Scrubbing the stain lightly with steel wool and then retreating as above will often lighten a bad scorch mark, but it'll probably make the fibres fuzz and could cause a hole.

Caution: Don't raise your hopes too high—disappointment is bad for your blood pressure.

Prevention: Iron delicate items first, not last, and don't press your luck trying to get rid of stubborn creases. Don't overdo the spray starch, and don't daydream while ironing!

Smoke/Soot (except tobacco smoke)

What is it? Tiny particles of oil and carbon that float in the air and land everywhere.

What can it do? Leave a black oily stain that's easy to spread, and has a strong, long-lasting odour. You might think you got rid of it six months ago, but it reappears with humid weather.

How hard? Can be difficult indeed on porous absorbent materials such as carpet, curtains, furniture, and unsealed brick and wood.

What to do first: As soon as you can see, decide whether it's something you want to tackle yourself. It it's a house fire, boiler blowup, or other major or minor calamity, your buildings insurance probably covers it, and your best bet is to let a smoke damage restoration contractor take care of it. If it's just a light smoke film from a woodstove, burned apple pie, or a stained fireplace front; or if you're determined to clean up your own disaster, start by removing the residue. Vacuum up any soot or ashes. Remove smoke film from hard surfaces (but not if painted with emulsion) with a duster dampened with turps.

What to do next: *Clothing:* Mist washable clothing with laundry pre-treatment (spray heavier on any visible smoke or soot stains), then launder in hot water, with bleach if safe for the fabric. Adding washing soda to the load will help cut the oily deposit.

If stains remain, repeat the procedure. Dry cleanables should be taken in for professional cleaning.

Carpet and upholstery: Seek professional advice.

Fireplaces: Scrub stone or brick with a stiff brush and a solution of one-half cup of powdered cold-water detergent per gallon of hot water. Apply plenty so it can float the smoke particles out, and then rinse. If your fireplace is really sooty, it may take several rounds. Apply Cuprinol Water Seal or Bourneseal after it's all good and dry to prevent further staining.

Walls and ceilings: Remove smoke film with dry sponges, then wash down with a sponge and sugar soap. Polish dry with a cotton terry cleaning cloth.

If that doesn't do it: Repainting, refinishing, or replacement will be required.

Prevention: Open the chimney damper before you open the oven door and before building a fire in the fireplace. Don't leave the meat browning while you go to answer the door—it may take longer than you think.

Soft Drinks

What is it? Sugar, colouring, flavourings, tannin in colas.

What can it do? Like any sugar spot, can become a permanent yellow stain if heat-set. The tannin and caramel colourings in dark-coloured drinks can also stain.

How hard? Easy when fresh, difficult if set.

What to do first: Take the time to rinse out the spill when it happens.

What to do next: *Fresh:* Blot out as much as possible with a clean cloth. Sponge the stain several times with warm (not hot) water. Make sure you get all the sugar out. Then launder washables;

feather the spot in dry cleanables and let it air dry.

Old/dry: Washables: Soak in enzyme detergent for 30 minutes to an hour and wash in warm water. *Dry cleanables:* Apply glycerine and leave for 30 minutes, then flush with warm water and feather.

If that doesn't do it: Let fabric dry; sponge with washing-up liquid and a few drops of vinegar. Flush with warm water, blot dry, and feather.

Caution: Don't iron or dry with heat until the sugar is completely removed.

Prevention: Don't drink while you drive or walk. Put the can down on a stable surface.

Soup

What is it? Meat juice, meat, vegetables, oils, maybe milk or cream, sugar (for tomato soup, see Tomato).

What can it do? Meat soups leave greasy stains that set with age; strongly-coloured soups such as borscht can leave vegetable dye stains.

How hard? Easy if you do it straight away; left to set, can be difficult—particularly meat soups. Because of the combination of ingredients, soup stains often call for a multi-pronged attack.

What to do first: Treat immediately by blotting up all you can with a dry cloth.

What to do next: *Fresh: Washables:* Sponge with warm water. apply laundry pre-treatment and let it sit for a few minutes, then wash in warm water. Air dry. If stain remains, soak in enzyme detergent for 30 minutes to an hour and wash again.

Dry cleanables: Sponge with enzyme detergent solution and a few drops of ammonia (no ammonia on silk or wool—use borax), then with cool water. If stain remains, apply paste of enzyme detergent (not on silk or wool), let it sit for 30 minutes without drying out, then rinse with water and feather.

Old/dry: Scrape to remove residue then treat as above.

Prevention: 'To ladle out' is almost synonymous with 'to spill.' And it's not only well-mannered to lean forward when you sip, it's clever stain prevention.

Soy Sauce, Worcestershire Sauce

What is it? Soy protein, salt, sugar, vinegar, colouring.

What can it do? Ruin clothes.

How hard? Difficult even when fresh; can be permanent if set by age or heat.

What to do first: Act **immediately**, if possible. Blot up all you can and sponge the spot with cool water.

What to do next: *Washables:* Sponge with mild vinegar solution. Apply laundry pre-treatment and wash in cool water. If stain remains, soak in enzyme detergent for 30 minutes to an hour and wash again.

Dry cleanables: Sponge with washing-up liquid and a few drops of vinegar, then rinse. If stain remains, apply paste of enzyme detergent and water (not on silk or wool), leave it on for 30 minutes without letting it dry, then rinse and feather.

Old/dry: Smear on glycerine and let it sit for 30 minutes to soften the stain, then treat as above.

If that doesn't do it: Take valuable pieces for expert spotting.

Caution: Don't use heat until you're sure it's gone.

Prevention: Don't trust the shaker nozzle to stay in place and don't shake too energetically.

Spaghetti sauce, red (see Ketchup)

Stickers (see Adhesives)

Suntan lotion (see Lotion)

Superglue (see Glue—Synthetic)

Sweets (other than chocolate)

What is it? Sugar, flavourings, dyes.

What can it do? The dyes used to colour sweets can make permanent stains. A sugar stain, if accidentally ironed, also makes a nasty yellow-brown spot.

How hard? Easy, unless dye stained or heat-set.

What to do first: Pry the child off it first, then scrape or pluck all you can from the surface.

What to do next: *Fresh:* For washables, soaking or laundering in warm water usually removes sweet stains. For dry cleanables, carpet, etc, sponge first with warm water, then with washing-up liquid solution and a few drops of vinegar. Finish by sponge-rinsing with water and feathering.

Old/dry: Virtually impossible to remove. Seek professional help.

If that doesn't do it: For washables, apply laundry pre-treatment and launder in warm water. For dry cleanables, take to cleaner.

Caution: Be sure all traces of the sugar are gone before ironing or hot-air drying.

Prevention: Don't give kids anything that can be half-eaten, then slipped under a cushion or left on the windowsill.

Sweets for the Neat

If you've reached the end of your liquorice rope and never want another peppermint holding the sofa cushions in place, ban your brood to the garden for snacks!

There are more and less messy sweets, so choose wisely. Any mum will tell you: Smarties over toffee, one-bite size over a bar of anything, avoid any sweet that squirts, turns your hands or mouth green, or is granular. Pass over anything marshmallow. Don't forget that no one's ever successfully sued the 'melt in your mouthers' for damage to their car seats. And if you pass out five ice lollies, demand five sticks in return. Don't stand in front of the gumball machine (with the children dressed in white) thinking, 'What can it hurt?' You know four goes in a row will turn out four bright colour-me-blue gumballs.

Tape (see Adhesives)

Tar

What is it? Asphalt waterproofing material, used on roofs, for paving, street mending, etc.

What can it do? Find its way to a door any distance from the car park, and leave black, black, black blobs and streaks that spread easily.

How hard? Depending on the dyes and other ingredients, can be very difficult to remove completely.

What to do first: Gently pluck or scrape as much of the tar off the surface as you can. Large, stubborn globs (as in carpet) can be frozen and shattered, like chewing gum. (See p. 000 and 000.)

What to do next: *Fresh:* Sponge repeatedly with white spirit until the black stain is completely removed. Work from the outside toward the centre, being careful not to spread the stain. If the stain has gone, dry the fabric, then apply laundry pre-treatment and launder washables in hot water if safe for the fabric. For carpet and upholstery, use a light, upward brushing motion, to pull the stain up and off the fibres; try not to rub it in deeper.

Old/dry: Take to dry cleaner.

If that doesn't do it: Take to dry cleaner.

Caution: Don't use water until you've removed as much as possible—water tends to set tar and make it spread even more.

Prevention: Speak strongly to whoever did it!

Tea (see Coffee)

Tobacco Smoke

What is it? Tiny particles of nicotine, tar and resins suspended in carbon dioxide, carbon monoxide, and other gases.

What can it do? Make life short for the puffer and miserable for the cleaner. The sticky particles settle on surfaces and build up into an ugly yellow-brown layer with a strong odour.

How hard? That filthy film of smoke is easy enough to remove from fabrics you can wash and surfaces you can scrub. But lingering odour can be a challenge, especially in car interiors, upholstered furniture, and carpet, where you can't reach all the particles trapped in padding materials, etc.

What to do first: Put up 'No Smoking' signs, so you won't have to do it again.

What to do next: *Washables:* Mist with laundry pre-treatment and wash in warm water. If odour remains, soak in mild vinegar solution and wash again.

Dry cleanables: Take for professional dry cleaning—you'll never get all the smoke odour out without cleaning the whole thing.

Hard surfaces: For walls and other water-safe surfaces, use a heavy-duty cleaner/degreaser in warm water. For windows with heavy smoke film, use sugar soap.

Upholstery: For upholstered furniture and car interiors, shampoo with rug and upholstery shampoo (if safe for the fabric). If the furniture isn't safe for wet-cleaning, have it professionally dry cleaned. *Note:* Odour will still linger in the padding and inaccessible areas of the fabric. Airing will help, but the only real cure is professional deodorising. Have carpet professionally steam cleaned, and ask for deodoriser to be added to the cleaning solution.

Prevention: See above.

Toilet cleaner (see Acid)

Tomato soup (see Tomato)

Tomato (fresh or canned tomatoes, tomato juice/sauce/purée, tomato soup)

What is it? One of the most popular flavours, and most common stains. At least it's easy to see! What you're dealing with here is tomatoes, plus salt, citric acid, and spices.

What can it do? Leave a reddish-brown blotch that will set with heat.

How hard? A bit reluctant when fresh; can be permanent if heat-set.

What to do first: Gently scrape and blot to remove all you can, being careful not to force the stain deeper into the fabric.

What to do next: *Washables:* Sponge with cool water, then with a solution of half vinegar and half water. Rinse with cool water. Apply a laundry pre-treatment and wash in warm water. Air dry. If stain remains, soak in enzyme detergent for 30 minutes to an hour and wash again.

Dry cleanables: Sponge with cool water, then with a solution of half vinegar and half water. Rinse with cool water. If stain remains, apply a paste of enzyme detergent and water (not on silk or wool), let it sit without drying out for up to 30 minutes, then rinse with water.

If that doesn't do it: Bleach with hydrogen peroxide.
Caution: Don't use hot water, hot-air drying, or iron until the stain has gone—heat will set it.
Prevention: Remember, no matter how slow it flows on tv ads, in real life it slops, splatters, and spreads like crazy. And don't ever imagine you can eat a tomato tidily: whole ones squirt, sliced ones drip and cherry tomatoes explode!

Tomato Ketchup, Spaghetti Sauce, Barbecue Sauce

What is it? Tomato, sugar, tannin, seasoning, possibly oil, maybe colouring.
What can it do? Season any clothes you own with a reddish-brown stain that will set with heat.
How hard? Takes some doing even when fresh; can become permanent if heat-set.
What to do first: Scrape and then blot to remove residue.
What to do next: *Fresh: Washables:* Sponge with cool water. Apply laundry pre-treatment, tamp if the fabric will tolerate it, and rinse. If stain goes, wash in warm water. If stain remains, sponge with a solution of half vinegar and half water, and rinse again. Reapply laundry pre-treatment and wash in warm water. *Dry cleanables:* Sponge with cool water and let dry. If stain remains, sponge with solution of half vinegar and half water, then rinse. *Old/dry:* Soften stain with warm glycerine and treat as above.
If that doesn't do it: Soak washables in enzyme detergent for 30 minutes to an hour and wash again. Apply paste of enzyme detergent and water to dry cleanables, let it sit 30 minutes without drying out, then rinse. As a last resort, bleach with hydrogen peroxide.
Caution: Don't use hot water, dry with heat, or iron, until the stain is gone—heat will set it.
Prevention: Get rid of nearly empty bottles so you won't have to beat on the bottom and splatter it around; don't put a puddle on your plate three times larger than you could ever consume. And when in Rome, wear a bib!

Toner (dry toner used in photocopiers)

What is it? Particles of carbon black or ink, often encased in tiny plastic spheres.

What can it do? Fly around everywhere, making smudges on clothing, carpet and furniture. Can result in very difficult stains if the ink escapes the plastic encapsulation.

How hard? If the plastic coating remains intact, it's just a very fine black dust that needs to be removed extra-cautiously. If the ink is released by a solvent, pressure, or heat, you've got a dye stain on your hands.

What to do first: Gently vacuum up all the toner possible, being careful not to rub it deeper into the fabric. The more you get out before applying any liquid, the better.

What to do next: *Washables:* Apply laundry pre-treatment, wash in cold water, and air dry. Check that all the toner has been removed before drying with heat or ironing. If stain remains, treat as for India ink.

Dry cleanables: Take to dry cleaners.

Caution: Don't use heat (hot water, hot dryer, or hot iron) until all traces of toner are gone.

Prevention: Follow the directions for adding toner, watch the repairman closely when he does it (he won't get toner on anything); or play stupid and let somebody else worry about that little 'add toner' indicator.

Typewriter ribbon (see Carbon Paper)

Unknown stains (see Mystery Stains)

Urine, animal or human (see Pet Stains)

Varnish (see Paint—Oil-Based)

Vegetables

What is it? What mothers like you to eat up, not spill or spread around. (Contains vegetable dye; possibly oil, tannin.)

What can it do? Attract rabbits, and leave a green or yellow stain.

How hard? Easy when fresh; harder as it ages.

What to do first: Blot or scrape to remove all you can.

What to do next: *Fresh:* Sponge with water. Apply laundry pre-treatment to washables and wash in warm water. Sponge dry cleanables with washing-up liquid and a few drops of vinegar, then rinse with water and feather. Air dry.

Old/dry: Treat as for fresh stain.

If that doesn't do it: Soak washables in enzyme detergent for 30 minutes to an hour, then launder in warm water. For dry cleanables, apply paste of enzyme detergent and water, let it sit 30 minutes without drying out, then rinse with warm water. If stain remains, sponge with methylated spirit and a few drops of vinegar (test first). Some vegetable stains may required bleaching.
Caution: Don't dry with heat or iron until the stain has gone—heat may set it.
Prevention: Always keep you eye on the family when you serve cabbage or anything similar. Move the high chair away from the wall, and wear an apron when you introduce the baby to sieved spinach.

Vomit

What is it? Acids, digestive enzymes, partially digested food (and often an indication that we overdid it).
What can it do? Stomach juices exist to digest, and when they get on carpet or clothes, they can 'eat' and damage fabrics, too! Vomit can also out do any deodorising spray in existence.
How hard? Upchuck is always unpleasant and untimely and on items not designed to be cleaned up quickly or easily. But you can get it out if you get to work at once. Left to set, vomit can cause permanent colour change.
What to do first: Quickly scrape and blot up all you can, then flush the spot with water to dilute the acids and prevent them from damaging the fabric. In carpet or upholstery, sponge on water liberally and blot it out.
What to do next: *Washables:* Soak the item in a solution of two pints warm water to one teaspoon washing-up liquid and two tablespoons of ammonia. Tamp or scrape to loosen the stain if the fabric will tolerate it. Rinse with cool water. If stain remains, soak in enzyme detergent 30 minutes to an hour, then launder in warm water. For coloured stains, use a bleach safe for the fabric.
Dry cleanables: For fabrics that will tolerate water, apply washing/up liquid and a few drops of ammonia (no ammonia on silk or wool). Tamp or scrape if fabric will tolerate it. Sponge-rinse with cool water. If stain remains, apply paste of enzyme detergent and water and leave it on there for 30 minutes, but don't let it dry out (not on silk or wool). Rinse with warm water and feather. As a last resort, bleach with hydrogen peroxide.

If that doesn't do it: It's probably a dye change caused by the acid—sorry!

Caution: Vomit must be spotted with water. If you have a vomit stain on a dry-cleanable fabric with low water tolerance, such as silk and taffeta, take it for professional spotting.

Prevention: Put the one who's always carsick in the front seat, and don't buy strongly coloured pet foods—the red dyes make for worse than usual vomit stains. Fido and Felix don't care what colour their food is, anyway—they're colour-blind.

Water Rings or White Marks on Furniture

What is it? A white ring or stain left on wood furniture by a wet glass or spilled liquid, or by heat. The heat or moisture chemically changes the finish and clouds it.

What can it do? Make your favourite furnishings look distinctly tacky, or even make you start crocheting doilies.

How hard? It can be as easy as fading away by itself, or as frustrating as a full-scale refinishing job.

What to do first: Wait a day or two before you do anything. The mark may lighten as absorbed moisture evaporates.

What to do next: Blemishes of this sort can usually be rubbed out using a mild abrasive mixed with a lubricant. Try one of these gentle combinations first: Rustin's Heat Damage Remover; Colron Wood Cleaner and Restorer; or cigarette ash and vegetable oil, mixed to a stiff paste and rubbed in. The idea is to gently rub the finish with the abrasive (along the grain of the wood) until the spot blends in with the surrounding area. Have patience, and don't be too anxious to move up to a stronger abrasive—it may scratch. When finished, reapply the wax or furniture polish you normally use to the spot.

If that doesn't do it: Go to a more aggressive abrasive, such as rottenstone (available in paint stores) in linseed or salad oil. Or, as a last resort, use T-Cut or polishing compound from a car accessory shop. There is danger with these of scratching or even rubbing right through the finish, so take it easy, and stop immediately if it appears the finish is growing thin. You'll definitely have to apply wax or polish to hide the dull area these abrasives will leave.

Prevention: On factory-finished furniture (which is usually lacquered), **use** that set of wildflower coasters. A coat of paste wax will help protect lacquered tabletops against damage. If you're finishing furniture yourself, use Dulux, Rustins or Silkens satin varnish or, on surfaces already coated with polyurethane varnish, use Colron Enhance acrylic varnish, all of which resist alcohol, heat, and moisture better.

Water Spots on Fabric

What is it? The stain everyone can afford. Water spots usually form on fabrics that contain sizing or finishing agents. The water displaces the sizing and is deposited around the edges of the spot in a ring or wavy line. Using water on dry cleanable fabrics without feathering the edge will often result in a water spot. Fabrics most susceptible to water spotting are taffeta, moiré, and hard-finished silk or rayon.
What can it do? Leave your favourite silk blouse looking as if it's been attacked by ringworm.
How hard? Comes out with washing or dry cleaning. Severe marks must be professionally treated.
What to do first: *Washables:* Wash the entire garment and dry as you would normally. *Dry cleanables:* Dampen the entire garment by waving it in the steam from a boiling kettle. If ironable, press while still damp, using a cloth. If the ring remains, you'll have to have the garment professionally dry cleaned.
Prevention: Stop trying to spot-clean silk and taffeta with water—it always leaves a water spot.

Water Stains on Ceilings

What is it? The result of water leaking down through a ceiling. The water carries dyes leached out of the roofing and insulation materials, and usually dries to a brown ring.
What can it do? Get you into the habit of lowering your gaze.
How hard? Can range from disguising a drip to the whole ceiling caving in.
What to do first: Try bleaching out the stain. This may remove it, if it's not too bad. Spray on a 1:5 mixture of liquid household bleach and water, or straight hydrogen peroxide.
What to do next: Small spots that still show can be covered by dabbing on a little white shoe polish.
If that doesn't do it: For large spots, seal the stain with pigmented

shellac (available at paint stores) or aluminium primer (not paint) and paint to match the surrounding area after the shellac dries. If you don't prime first, the stain will bleed through the paint.
Prevention: Mend the roof **before** the autumn rains. And make sure you know where the central heating pipes are before you start knocking nails into the floor.

Wax (candle wax, paraffin, crayon, etc)

What is it? Wax, possibly dye and perfume.
What can it do? The dyes in candles and crayons can cause permanent stains. And since it drips on while molten, the hot wax from a candle penetrates deep!
How hard? One of the tougher ones, and if the wax contains strong dye (such as red) it can be a real challenge.
What to do first: For candle drips, first freeze the wax to harden it (see p. 52). Then you can shatter the brittle mass by striking it briskly with the handle of a butter knife, and gently scrape to remove as much of the remaining residue as possible. Be careful not to distort or damage fibres.
What to do next: *Washables:* After removing the bulk of the wax by freezing, place the stained area between two pieces of clean white cotton cloth or white paper towels. Iron with a warm iron to melt the wax and force it into the blotters. Change blotters and carry on ironing until all the wax is gone. Apply laundry pre-treatment and wash in hot water. Use bleach if safe for the fabric.

Dry cleanables: After you've removed all you can by freezing, iron between blotters as above, take for professional cleaning to remove residue.

Hard surfaces: Crayon can be removed from painted walls, wood, wallpaper, floors, and most hard surfaces with WD-40; just spray and wipe.

If that doesn't do it: Spray with WD-40 and let sit a few minutes. Tamp, then apply laundry pre-treatment and launder washables in hot water if safe for the fabric. Remove WD-40 from dry cleanables with K2r Stain Remover Spray.

Prevention: Put a tablecloth under candles if you really treasure your tabletop; buy dripless candles and don't leave windows open or fans running nearby, even so.

Take the time to find washable crayons and don't give out crayons to amuse visiting kids!

Wine (red, rosé; for white wine, see Alcohol)

What is it? Alcohol, fruit, sugar, tannin.

What can it do? Leave you with a red nose and permanent purple stains. The sugar in wine can also set with age and heat into a stubborn yellow spot.

How hard? Tough to very tough, depending on the wine and the fabric and how many mornings after it takes you to notice it. Aged stains can be impossible, especially if set by heat.

What to do first: Blot to remove as much as possible, and immediately sponge with cool water until no more colour is being removed. For sturdy fabrics, rub table salt into the stain, and treat with the boiling water method (see Fruit—Red). For fabrics that won't tolerate boiling water, follow the procedures below.

What to do next: *Washables:* Sponge with washing-up liquid and a few drops of vinegar. Rinse with cool water. If stain remains, apply laundry pre-treatment and wash in cool water; air dry. If stain remains, soak in enzyme detergent for 30 minutes to an hour and rewash in warm water.

Dry cleanables: Sponge with washing-up liquid and a few drops of vinegar as long as any wine colour is being removed. Rinse with cool water. If stain remains, apply paste of enzyme detergent and water (not on silk or wool), let sit for 30 minutes without drying out, then rinse with water. Feather to avoid water spots.

If that doesn't do it: Bleach with as strong a bleach as the fabric

181

will tolerate. Valuable pieces should be taken in for expert spotting and cleaning.

Caution: Don't use hot water, dry with heat, or iron before you're sure it's gone—heat will set sugar stains. Don't use soap.

Prevention: Put the cork in the bin or the ash tray—not on the tablecloth. Practise until you can pour like a wine waiter—slowly, twisting the bottle neck to the side as you finish (so any drips end up inside).

Wood Stain

What is it? Pigments and dyes in a solvent or water-emulsion base.

What can it do? Live up to its name. Talk about a stain—this was created to colour things, and that's what it does—usually permanently.

How hard? The worst—if it's on something porous, you aren't likely to get it out.

What to do first: Don't let it dry! If you can flush it out while it's still wet, there's chance of complete removal. If you let it dry, it's probably a lost cause.

What to do next: Treat oil-based stain as under Paint—Oil-Based, water-based stain as under Paint—Water-Based.

If that doesn't do it: Treat as a Dye stain.

Prevention: Make sure all furniture legs have glides or rubber or plastic cups, and you won't have wood stain leaching out of furniture legs on to carpet. And if you have to put furniture on to freshly cleaned carpet, place a square of plastic, foil, or unprinted carboard under the legs until the carpet is completely dry.

Worcestershire sauce (see Soy Sauce)

Yellowing of laundry (see Chapter 2)

Acknowledgements

Writing about stains takes as many 'helps' as removing them. My sincere thanks to all the stain crew:

Gary Luke, executive editor of New American Library, for the original idea and for his selfless exploration of stain possibilities.

Mark Browning, my partner and cleaning consultant, who cut through the terrifying thicket of technical questions that surround stain removal.

Carol Cartaino, my agent and worst taskmaster (and owner of more stainables than Bloomingdale's).

Tobi Haynes, my production manager, who fed it all into the computer and saw that it all happened on time.

Craig LaGory, the illustrator, who stays awake at night creating splotch monsters.

Della Gibbs and **Linda Hegg**, researchers, who helped crack some of the more elusive stain removal mysteries.

Maytag, for their excellent information on fabrics and their care.

Procter & Gamble, Unilever, Johnson Wax, R. R. Street & Co., many other manufacturers, and the **Soap & Detergent Association**, for help in understanding their specific stain-removal products and strategies.

The many helpful launderers, dry cleaners and **carpet cleaners**, who spent time sharing the tricks of their trade with me.

And I wouldn't want to forget the fast food companies who made it all necessary, and the manufacturers of anything red.

The publishers would also like to thank the **Fabric Care Research Association**, Knaresborough Road, Harrogate, for their expert help during production of the Ebury Press edition.

Index